STONEHENGE

WONDERS OF THE WORLD

....

STONEHENGE

ROSEMARY HILL

Harvard University Press
Cambridge, Massachusetts
2008

Copyright © Rosemary Hill 2008

Printed in the United States of America

First published in the United Kingdom in 2008 by
Profile Books
3A Exmouth House
Pine Street
London ECIR OJH

        Library of Congress Cataloging-in-Publication Data
Hill, Rosemary.
  Stonehenge / Rosemary Hill.
      p. cm.
  "First published in the United Kingdom by Profile Books"—T.p. verso.
  Includes bibliographical references and index.
  ISBN-13: 978-0-674-03132-6 (alk. paper)
1. Stonehenge (England).
2. Megalithic monuments—England—Wiltshire. 3. Wiltshire (England)—
Antiquities. 4. Stonehenge (England)—Historiography. I. Title.
  DA142.H55 2008
  082 s—dc22
  [936.2'319]   2008012024

For
Christopher Logue
'Cyclops Christianus'

CONTENTS

INTRODUCTION

'The rational reader, if he is interested in the history of ideas, must be willing to hear about all ideas which in their time have been potent to move men.'

Frances Yates, *The Art of Memory*

The desire for knowledge and the love of mystery are two of the most powerful human impulses and Stonehenge satisfies both at once. That is why it has never lost its hold on our imagination or our curiosity. It is the most famous megalithic structure in the world, instantly recognisable from the sketchiest of outlines and visited by over half a million people a year. Yet after more than a millennium of speculation and investigation we still have no certain idea of what it is or why it was built. By 1695 the antiquary Edmund Gibson was already complaining that Stonehenge is 'so singular and receives so little light from history that almost every one has advanced a new notion'. Three hundred years later there has been considerably more light and many more notions, but few secure answers.

This book, unusually in the vast literature on the subject, supports no particular theory about the purpose and meaning of prehistoric Stonehenge. It is concerned instead with what the monument is, physically, and what it has meant throughout historic time to those who have considered it, from medieval monks to modern archaeologists. Stonehenge today is their creation. It is a work of art and science, of poetry, astronomy and literature that reflects back to us the centuries that have passed over it. Inigo Jones saw in it a Platonic ideal of architecture. Wordsworth heard echoes of the French Revolutionary wars, while to Charles Darwin it offered a case study in the activity of earthworms. It has been a focus of counter-cultural protest and a once and future symbol of Arthurian romance. These and many other images have sunk deep into our collective memory and travelled on through space and time until today Stonehenge is to be seen in many places far from Salisbury Plain. There are replica or tribute henges from western Nebraska to New Zealand and in other, less expected ways Stonehenge is a transforming presence. In the sculpture of Henry Moore and the planning of Georgian Bath, from William Blake's *Jerusalem* to the shopping centre at Milton Keynes, its influence is felt. It is, not least, an ancestor of the modern traffic roundabout.

The stones have had a rich but far from peaceful history. So many ideas to so few facts makes for an unstable compound and the struggle for intellectual ownership has not always been dignified. History, notoriously, is written by the winners and the overall winners in the academic struggle for the stones have been the archaeologists. Understandably their interest concentrates on those who have most obviously paved the way for modern archaeological understanding and they are inclined to rate their predecessors according to how 'right' they were. The seventeenth-century antiquary William Stukeley is usually praised for his surveying work but taken severely to task for his Druidic theories. Inigo Jones, who thought Stonehenge was Roman, is written off entirely, while Turner's great watercolour view of 1829 gets marked down for inaccuracy. But Stonehenge does not belong to archaeology, or not to archaeology alone. In the chapters that follow we make an appropriately circular tour of the stones, beginning and ending with archaeological interpretations, but looking at them, in between, from different angles to see how they have appeared to antiquaries, architects, astronomers and others. There is no attempt to include every reference ever made to Stonehenge. The purpose is to concentrate instead on those accounts that have had the power to move others, whether by art or by argument. Sometimes what is least 'correct' may be most influential. Aylett Sammes's seventeenth-century account of Stonehenge was described, quite fairly, by his contemporaries as 'ignorant' and 'silly', yet it lives today in cult cinema. The Wicker Man haunts the imagination of many thousands who have never heard of Sammes himself.

Ideas, however wrong or loosely based in history or science, if they are believed for long enough will usually break through into reality and they have done so often at Stonehenge. In 1985, when there was a confrontation between police and supporters of the Stonehenge Free Festival, it was reported in the press that police were stationed to watch for trouble at the points where local ley lines intersected. Ley lines are said to mark ancient alignments along which psychic energy flows, but whatever they had or had not been in the past, the leys now came to exert a measurable effect on events. Nowhere has this principle been more fully demonstrated than in the case of the Druids, who have haunted Stonehenge, to the fury of archaeologists, for over two and a half centuries. Stuart

Piggott, one of the most distinguished archaeologists to work at Stonehenge and one of the most important historians of the Druids, could barely contain his fury with their modern counterparts. Among their ranks, he wrote witheringly, 'many a psychological misfit and lonely crank' has found a home. This is no way to describe Winston Churchill or Queen Elizabeth II, both of whom were initiated as Druids and such contempt seems quite unnecessary. It is true that the original, Iron Age, Druids could not possibly have built Stonehenge. It is also true that modern Druids cannot trace their origins back with any clarity further than the eighteenth century. But two hundred and fifty years is a substantial pedigree, longer indeed than that of archaeology, which is a largely Victorian discipline. Druids therefore find a place in every chapter of this book except the first.

In so far as Stonehenge has been a mirror of changing times it has thrown back a challenging and often far from flattering image. Deeply held beliefs in human progress, civil rights and the steady march of knowledge have run up against the stones and not always survived. While time has yielded greater understanding it has not always brought deeper appreciation or respect. It is still less than a century since Stonehenge was put up for sale at a local auction and knocked down for £6,600. It has been chipped at by sightseers, dug up by archaeologists (some more careful than others), overflown by the army, spray-painted, invaded and now stands hemmed in by traffic on two main roads. At the time of writing its future is, yet again, in dispute and under review. But if all this is depressing it is the dark side of what makes Stonehenge thrilling, the fact that after five thousand years it is still alive, still an object of passion. Most monuments, after a century or two, are respectfully moth-balled, visited, guidebook in hand, to satisfy an academic interest or pass an idle afternoon. At Stonehenge scholarship and worship are still part of its daily existence. Within the last fifteen years archaeologists have redated the stone circle twice, radically changing our understanding of it, and currently the Stonehenge Riverside Project, which involves the largest research team ever assembled, is turning up new information year by year. In 1999, after more than a decade of sometimes violent dispute, Stonehenge was the occasion of a House of Lords ruling that set a legal precedent and allowed those who wish to celebrate or simply visit at the summer solstice to enter freely. They come in their tens of thousands. It is there, close in among the stones, that all the other questions fall away. Stonehenge is an overwhelming presence, a masterpiece of art and engineering in which gigantic force and minute delicacy combine; its beauty and strangeness abide.

. . . .

A VERY SHORT PREHISTORY

'Incontrovertible facts are luxuries in prehistoric research.'

Aubrey Burl

What we now call Stonehenge stands on Salisbury Plain in Wiltshire at Latitude 51° 11' North, Grid Reference SU 122 421 on the Ordnance Survey. Its site today is a triangle of 46.9 acres bounded on two sides by roads, the A303 and A344, and on the third by the Larkhill Track. It is owned by the state and administered by English Heritage, a government-funded agency. At this point we come, almost, to the end of the uncontested facts. This greatest of all British stone circles has been, for many centuries, a ruin, but a ruin of what exactly nobody knows. To work your way through the vast literature on Stonehenge is rather like looking at it on a satellite photograph. At first the subject is too distant to be made out. Then, as the magnification increases, everything comes briefly into focus, before dissolving again in a blur of detail and dispute. This chapter gives a brief account of what is most generally believed, at the time of writing, to be the history of the physical monument itself in the prehistoric period. Although I will point out the areas that are particularly contentious, there is almost nothing in what follows that would not be disputed by somebody. As for the question of why Stonehenge was built, exactly who by and what for, the short answer is that nobody knows. The many other longer answers and their implications are the subject of the rest of the book.

To begin with, let us imagine Stonehenge away for a moment and visualise Salisbury Plain as it looked in the Neolithic or late Stone Age, about 3000 BC. This was already a populated and largely man-made landscape of brownish-yellow chalk downland. Most of the once dense woodland had been cleared. Near the place that would become Stonehenge there is evidence that wooden posts, perhaps with some ritual significance, were raised as long ago as the Mesolithic period, between 8500 and 6700 BC. Three and a half millennia later, by the time the monument was begun, its site was surrounded by long barrows, seventeen or so of them within three miles. These large communal graves, earth mounds raised over stone or wooden burial chambers, were originally faced with chalk and would once have gleamed brilliant white, but by the late Neolithic the earliest of them was more than a thousand years old. They were passing out of use when work on Stonehenge started. There were other constructions too. On a low ridge about two and a half miles to the north-west of the site was what is now called Robin Hood's Ball, an earthwork of interrupted concentric banks and ditches, its purpose unclear. More recent, and just about 875 yards north of the Stonehenge site was the earthwork known as the Cursus, from the Latin for racetrack. This is a pair of banks, about 100 yards apart and running over a mile and half. To its north-west lies another, smaller, cursus, no longer visible on the ground. Whatever these cursus forms were, they were not racetracks. Their true purpose is one of

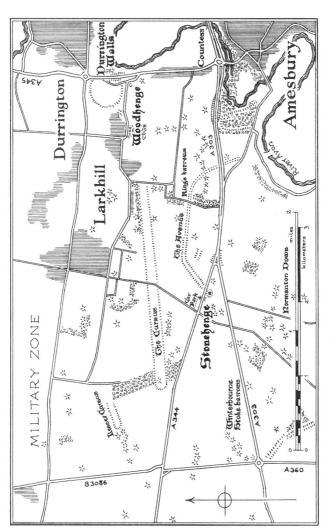

1. Stonehenge and the surrounding area.

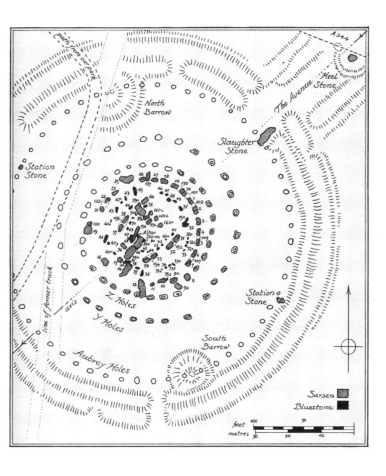

2. A plan of the central part of the monument showing the numbering of the
stones established by Flinders Petrie in 1880, as used in the text here.

the few Stonehenge mysteries to which hardly anybody has claimed to know the answer.

Salisbury Plain today is a landscape on which death has left more obvious traces than everyday life, but the people who inhabited it can be identified as a settled farming community. They were genetically identical to ourselves if rather shorter – the men about five feet five and the women five feet two – and usually shorter-lived. They kept cattle, pigs, sheep and dogs and grew cereal and other crops. They made pottery, used tools, fashioned arrowheads from flint, wove cloth and made rope, and their world was not entirely bounded by the limits of the plain. Widening the picture further, the people and the monuments of Wessex take their place in the broader landscape of Neolithic north-western Europe. In Brittany there were comparable burial mounds, some of them older than the British ones. At Carnac the great stone rows and circles had already stood for eight hundred years. Across what archaeologists call the Atlantic zone, from Brittany to the coast of Ireland and up to Orkney and the Hebrides, megalithic architecture spread and developed local variations. The Neolithic village of Scara Brae on Orkney, the standing stones of Callanish on Lewis and the monuments of Carnac have elements in common with Stonehenge and the structures near it, though none is identical. Exactly which cross-currents of influence flowed most strongly to and from Salisbury Plain is a much debated matter.

For Stonehenge itself, however, everyone agrees that there was no exact precedent, nor indeed, it seems, was there anything like it ever again. The monument as a whole was constructed over fourteen or fifteen hundred years, the work of seventy generations. How much if anything the last builders knew of the intentions of the first is impossible to guess. Nor is it clear why, when work began, they chose this particular site. It lies on a slight, north-easterly slope, in neither a prominent position nor an obviously easy one on which to build, yet the choice can scarcely have been random. This must have already been a place of some significance. The long and complex process of construction is divided by archaeologists into three phases. Phase One was a simple earthwork, a circular ditch with an internal bank and a small outer bank or counterscarp. It was dug in sections with picks made from antlers, which were discarded when the work was done, and it is from them that carbon-dating sets it at about 3000–2920 BC, one of the few nearly precise and undisputed dates available. When it was finished this chalk-white and almost perfect circle measured 331 feet in diameter, with several breaks which might be called entrances. The largest was to the north-east, with another smaller one to the south and a possible third at the south-west. As well as the casually discarded picks, the ditch contained some deliberately buried cattle bones. These were already ancient when they were laid there and might be what we would call relics, objects imbued with significance.

The most recent research confirms that this first phase also included the digging of the fifty-six pits inside the bank which came to be known as the Aubrey Holes. It is thought that at first they held wooden posts. Later they were filled and became the repositories for cremated human bone. Now marked with concrete plaques and ignored by most visitors, they remain one of the most mysterious and discussed features of the monument.

Phase Two began in the late Neolithic age before about

2400 BC against a background of more general social change and expansion. Between these first two phrases there may have been a period when Stonehenge was neglected and abandoned, but the evidence is not conclusive and the most recent findings make it seem less likely that the monument ever fell out of use. By the time work recommenced there were more people living in the area and they were keeping more livestock. They also had new styles of pottery. The incised jars known as Grooved Ware began to appear and 'henge' monuments – that is, banks and ditches enclosing elaborate timber constructions – were multiplying. To the south-east of Stonehenge was Coneybury, built in about 2700 BC, while to the north-east lay Woodhenge, as it came to be called, which dates from around 2300 BC, and the much larger henge, known as Durrington Walls, which is about two hundred years older. At Stonehenge itself there is evidence of a great deal of timber construction. Posts were erected inside and outside the earthwork. Whether they formed structures, and if so of what sort, or whether they were independent posts, something like those from the Mesolithic period, is a matter on which archaeologists are divided, although the case for structures is clearer round the edge of the monument. At some point a substantial fence or palisade was built to the north-west, while gradually over time the original ditch was allowed to silt up and many cremated remains were buried. The purpose of this second Stonehenge might fairly be described as a cremation cemetery. Of the first Stonehenge and its use, its relationship to Durrington Walls and the light it casts on the possible meaning of both, there will be more to say in a later chapter.

But whatever Stonehenge was by now, four hundred

years or more after construction began, it was nothing like the picture on the front of this book or indeed anything that most people would associate with the name. It was only in Phase Three that the stones arrived, and with the coming of the big 'sarsen' stones and the smaller 'bluestones' the monument we recognise today took shape. Sarsen is an immensely hard sandstone that occurs in large surface deposits on the Marlborough Downs and is known locally as greywether for its resemblance to sheep. It is from there that many people believe the Stonehenge sarsens were brought. The bluestones are smaller and more mysterious. They are mostly about six feet six inches long and are a medley of dolerite, rhyolites and volcanic ash not local to Salisbury Plain. It is generally agreed that they came from at least ten different sources in the Mynydd Preseli area of South Wales, from where most archaeologists and anthropologists believe they were brought to the site by people. There is, however, a fiercely argued minority view that they arrived naturally by glaciation in the ice age. Some of the bluestones have been worked like the sarsens into lintels with sockets and one has a groove down its side. Clearly they had been used before for another structure and may have been set up at one time as a miniature Stonehenge either there or elsewhere.

At what date all the stones arrived, in what order they were erected, moved and re-erected, and over what period of time are not only uncertain but some of the questions under energetic review at the time of writing. Archaeology, which traditionally likes to divide its subjects into three phases, has found it necessary to divide Phase Three of Stonehenge into two separate sets of sub-phases, 3i, 3ii and 3iii, as well as 3a, 3b and 3c. What is generally agreed is that with the arrival of the stones the site was reoriented. The axis was shifted by three degrees to the south-east, where it aligns with the rising sun at midsummer and the sunset at midwinter. It seems that some bluestones and some sarsens came first, with what is now known as the Heel Stone perhaps the earliest in place, followed by the rectangle of Station Stones. The bluestones were set up next, possibly in pairs in two concentric arcs. The holes where they stood in this phase are now known as the Q and R holes. These are no longer visible and give an ambiguous impression of what this formation, later dismantled, was like and how many stones were in it. Next came the sarsens, carried probably on some kind of sledge and erected perhaps with the use of staged platforms.

Nobody knows whether the stone monument was ever completed. Sarsen stone 11 is far too small to have supported a lintel, and this suggests to some archaeologists that the builders ran out of big stones and the work was never finished. If it was completed, Stonehenge would have consisted of an outer circle of thirty upright sarsens, evenly spaced except where stones 1 and 30 stand further apart, as if to emphasise the north-eastern entrance. Across the top of them and held in place by mortise and tenon joints were lintels which would have formed a continuous ring, linked with tongue and groove joints. These are timber construction techniques. Stonehenge is a timber building imitated in stone. Inside the sarsen ring there stood a matching circle of bluestones, and within this double circle stood the five great free-standing three-stone structures, shaped like doorways and known as trilithons. They made up a horseshoe, with, inside them, a matching formation of bluestones. There were other stones as well, within and beyond the central monument, and these have, over later centuries, acquired names which recollect the myths and theories that have gathered about Stonehenge. Their naming belongs to later chapters. Most famous and disputed is the Heel Stone, a great sarsen boulder 16 feet high, that stands outside the circle, leaning towards its centre. There is a ditch around it and it was originally one of a pair. At the entrance to the circle, half submerged, lies the Slaughter Stone, which once stood upright with, perhaps, two companions, one on either side. Near the centre, crushed under the fallen upright and lintel of the central Great Trilithon, lies the Altar Stone, a huge piece of Cosheton Bed sandstone from Preseli. Beyond the circle and within the bank, close to its edge, stand, or stood, the four Station Stones, marking out a rectangle. Two of them, small sarsens, survive, the sites of the other two are marked by low mounds known as the North and South Barrows.

The stones at the centre of the monument have all been shaped. Sarsen is immensely hard and it had to be worked with stone mauls or hammers. The mauls, held in leather slings, were whirled and slung at the surface with force. Even so the shaping and tooling must have been laborious. Then there was the business of getting the stone uprights the same height to keep the lintels horizontal, which was much more difficult, especially on a slope, than cutting wood to length. Probably the builders used plumb lines and they could certainly have made effective spirit levels using water. Even so, some of the uprights were balanced precariously in holes too shallow to support them. The first to fall may have come down in prehistoric times. There were other mistakes. Lintel 156 has two little mortise holes on the top side which indicate a false start. The bluestones within the trilithons were set up first as an oval, which was only later opened up into a horseshoe. It was probably at this point in the last phase of stone building, that the approach road, the great Avenue was constructed. It is a broad earthwork with a low bank and ditch on either side and it runs from the entrance along a curving course for a mile and three-quarters down to the River Avon.

Until very recently this stone construction phase was thought to have taken place over a period from about 2550 to 2300 BC, but current research suggests that these stages were both earlier and more rapid, that the sarsens were in place by 2400 BC at the latest and possibly two centuries earlier. The rearrangement of the bluestones and the building of the Avenue are currently thought to date from around 2280–1930 BC. In about 1600 BC two more rings of holes, now called the Y and Z holes, were dug. This last addition seems never to have served any function, the holes never contained posts or stones or ashes, and after them no more work took place at Stonehenge. At some point, probably after the upright sarsens were in position, at least eight of them were carved with images of axes and a dagger. Some time between 2400 and 2140 BC the body of a young man who had apparently been killed by arrows, and is now known as the Stonehenge Archer, was buried in the main ditch. These flickers of activity strike the only sparks in the surrounding darkness of the prehistoric record.

It is impossible to know how long the site remained in use after the Y and Z holes were dug but perhaps not long. In the fourteen hundred years of its construction the landscape around Stonehenge and the culture it supported had changed profoundly. The latest date thought possible for the Y holes is 1520 BC and by then the Neolithic had given way to the

Bronze Age. The plain was much more intensively farmed. There were permanent field systems and settlements. Indeed it would have required a relatively large population, able to survive by only seasonal labour, to find the workforce and the time to build the stone stage of Stonehenge. A recent calculation of the labour involved suggested that the raising of the lintels would have taken a team of twenty men a hundred and forty-five days. They must also have been highly organised and so, perhaps, a hierarchical society was emerging. Certainly it was more individualistic. By the time metal and so-called Beaker Ware (the pottery associated with a late-neolithic western European culture)begin to be found, the long barrows were being replaced by round barrows, centred on single graves. The communal traditions of the last two thousand years were breaking down. By now the view from within the stones embraced a skyline punctuated by newer barrows, including those at Normanton Down and the King Barrow Ridge, while away beyond the horizon lay Silbury Hill, which dates from 2700 BC, and the great stone circle at Avebury, one of the largest in Britain, built, probably, between the first and second phases of Stonehenge. At Winterbourne Stoke, to the south-west, lies what the archaeologist Julian Richards calls the 'final great cemetery', a spectacular group of barrows of every type whose history encompasses the whole period of the building of Stonehenge.

How long the site retained its resonance or any of its intended meaning we cannot know. After the Middle Bronze Age the physical history of Stonehenge is one of disuse and dilapidation as stones fell or were removed, and roads, rabbits and farming all took their toll until the twentieth century, when restoration work began. All of this belongs to what

3. Aerial view, courtesy of SacredSites.com, showing the path for tourists and the A344 which runs just behind the Heel Stone.

follows. But before passing from prehistory into history it is perhaps worth pausing to reflect that the Stonehenge described here is in some important ways, both physically and intellectually, a work not of the Neolithic and Bronze Ages, but of the present. Strictly speaking, the sight that greets the visitor today is less than half a century old, dating back no further than 1964, which was when the stones were last moved. Only seven of the twenty-five remaining uprights and two of the lintels are still as originally placed. The rest have been lifted and repaired at least once. Stone 60 has been substantially filled and many of the rest are set in twentieth-century concrete.

As for the mental pictures of Stonehenge formed by successive ages, if they were captured and run in sequence like a film they would show almost the opposite of what is described here. The great sarsens would come first, the Aubrey Holes only much later. The full length of the Avenue would appear, vanish for two hundred years and be rediscovered by other means. The earliest post constructions would be seen almost last and all the pictures might seem to go in slow motion until, in the last sixty years or so, they speed up and a succession of quickly changing snapshots flickers past. As recently as the mid-1990s Stonehenge took a great leap backwards in time when it was found to be a whole millennium older than had been thought and changed abruptly from a Bronze Age to an almost entirely Neolithic structure. By 2001 respected archaeologists were talking of the need to 'reinvent' Stonehenge, and their latest findings have not only made the stone circle older, again, but thereby placed it in a different cultural landscape.

Meanwhile the figures that have inhabited this imaginative

scene, the supposed builders of Stonehenge, have been a mixed and sometimes raucous crowd. Saxons have alternated with Romans and Danes. The Beaker People have appeared, vanished again and now hang tentatively around the edge, while the Druids first moved in over three centuries ago and have never left, despite the best endeavours of archaeologists to shoo them away. Such, then, is the nature of the ancient monument from which this book takes its departure and of the modern one to which in due course it will return.

2

CONTENDING WITH OBLIVION:
THE ANTIQUARIES

*'These antiquities are so exceeding old that no Books doe reach
them so there is no way to retrieve them but by comparative
antiquitie ... writ upon the Spott.'*

John Aubrey

After about 1600 BC, when work stopped on the construction of Stonehenge, there follow more than two millennia of
silence. Prehistory turned into history without shedding any
recorded light on Salisbury Plain. None of the Roman historians mentions the monument – an omission into which great
significance has sometimes later been read – and the Venerable Bede said nothing about it either. It is first glimpsed
in history in a deed of 937, when 'Stanheyeg' features as a
boundary marker for the land given by King Athelstan to the
abbey of Wilton. Otherwise for Stonehenge, the Dark Ages
are dark indeed. It is only after the Norman Conquest that
details begin to emerge. In Henry of Huntingdon's *Historia
Anglorum*, written in about 1130, 'Stanenges' is listed as one of
the wonders of the country, but 'no one can conceive', Henry
notes, 'how such great stones have been so raised aloft, or why
they were built here'. Nor was anybody sure about the exact

meaning of the name. '*Stan*' comes from the Old English for 'stone', but whether 'heng', or 'henge' or 'henges' as it variously appears from now on, derives from hinge or hanging place, or whether it refers to the construction or the shape of the trilithons, which resemble an early English gallows, remains, like much else, uncertain. In medieval Latin it became Chorea Gigantum, meaning Giants' Dance or Ring.

Many of Henry of Huntingdon's questions were answered, in what he considered suspiciously ample detail, by his contemporary Geoffrey of Monmouth. Geoffrey's *Historia Regum Britanniae*, or *The History of the Kings of Britain*, covers the period from the founding of Britain by Brutus through the rise of successive dynasties to its decline after the Saxon invasion. The story of Brutus, a Trojan descendant of Aeneas, from whose name 'Britain' was said to derive, was one of the medieval foundation myths to recur in connection with Stonehenge. The other is the tale of Joseph of Arimathea. Joseph, in whose tomb Christ was buried, was said to have come to England after the resurrection, bringing with him twelve apostles and, it was later believed, the Holy Grail, the cup used at the Last Supper. There he built the first Christian church at Glastonbury. By the fifteenth century, in Malory's *Morte d'Arthur*, Joseph, Glastonbury and the Grail had all become interwoven with the Arthurian legends and together they continue to haunt Stonehenge, but the process began with Geoffrey, whose book is the main source of the Arthurian stories as well as that of King Lear. His Stonehenge became the burial place of Uther Pendragon, having been built by King Aurelius as a monument to the Britons murdered there by the treacherous Saxon Hengist. The story of the massacre was already recorded in the early ninth-century *Historia Britonnum*, a work often credited to the Welsh monk Nennius. Geoffrey elaborated it, however, as he did much else. He explained that Aurelius was advised by Merlin to bring over a Giants' Ring from Mount Killaraus in Ireland, which feat was eventually accomplished with the help of the wizard's magic skills. The source for all this new information was, apparently, an ancient book borrowed from his friend Walter the Archdeacon. The book was never produced and Henry of Huntingdon was not the only sceptic. In 1190 William of Newburgh complained of Geoffrey that 'everything this man wrote … was made up'. Yet whether by coincidence or through some faint echo of received tradition, his account is not entirely fabulous. The idea that the stones, or some of them, were brought from the west was proved to be true in the last century and another of Geoffrey's claims was revived in the present one. Merlin, he said, had recommended the Giants' Ring for its healing properties. Baths prepared at the foot of the stones with water that had washed over them would, apparently, heal wounds. Nine hundred years later, in December 2006, the *Guardian* newspaper ran the headline, 'Stonehenge was a Hospital', over a story about a paper presented by Professors Geoffrey Wainwright and Timothy Darvill to the Society of Antiquaries, arguing that the bluestones were indeed brought to Wessex for their supposed healing properties.

The visual record for the Middle Ages is also sparse. Two depictions survive in illuminated manuscripts of the fourteenth century, while a fifteenth-century drawing discovered recently in Douai in France is notable for showing four standing trilithons and for clearly indicating the pegs inserted into the lintels. The first detailed depiction of Stonehenge

4. One of the earliest images of Stonehenge, this drawing comes from a Scala Mundi, or Chronicle of the World, of about 1440–41. It shows four standing trilithons and clearly indicates their pegged construction.

to survive is a watercolour, now in the British Museum, by Lucas de Heere. De Heere was a Flemish artist who lived in London from 1567 to 1577 and seems to have made another, less distinguished, contribution to the subject by carving his name on sarsen 53. Meanwhile, despite doubts about its reliability, *The History of the Kings of Britain* remained popular and its account of Stonehenge was repeated by other authors. Only with the Renaissance, the revival of classical scholarship and the dawn of the New Learning towards the end of the fifteenth century, did it begin to fall out of favour, for the nature of history writing itself was changing. England's next great historian, Polydore Vergil, had no time for old 'monkish' texts, which were, he thought, for the most part 'bald, uncouth, chaotic and deceitful'. Vergil, whose *Anglia Historia* was first published in Basel in 1534 and dedicated to Henry VIII, was an Italian priest who came to England in 1502. He wrote his history methodically, on the basis of critical comparison of the documentary sources, and he was caustic about Geoffrey of Monmouth, whom he accused of 'moste impudent lyeing'. There were patriotic complaints that Vergil was 'polutynge oure Englyshe chronicles … with his Romishe lyes', but the argument was lost. History from now on required documents and so Stonehenge, for which there were none, disappeared from history as abruptly as it had arrived.

Nearly a century passed before another sort of enquiry, antiquarianism, began to shed some light on it. Antiquaries were a relatively new intellectual species, largely a product of the Reformation, and they were interested in what could be discovered of the past by looking beyond the written records. They studied anything that was old – stones, metal, pottery, coins – attracting in the process much derision from contemporaries who thought it an 'unnaturall disease' to be so 'enamour'd of old age and wrinkles'. Yet the antiquaries were the first archaeologists. They were also the first oral historians, costume historians, art historians and folklorists. They opened up vast intellectual horizons and if, as later archaeologists have sometimes been quick to point out, they made mistakes, they were not alone in that and, working in an age before academic specialisation, before science and the arts had parted company, they were also able to make daring and useful connections.

It was James I, who prided himself on being up to date with intellectual fashion, who initiated the archaeological investigation of Stonehenge, although as befits the man known as 'the wisest fool in Christendom' his efforts had mixed results. Staying nearby at Wilton House in 1620, he expressed an interest in the stones. Since the Reformation the land on which Stonehenge stood had passed into private hands and it was to remain private property until the twentieth century. James's intimate friend the Duke of Buckingham, eager to please, immediately tried to buy it for the King. The owner, however, refused to sell, so Buckingham had to be content with digging an enormous hole in the middle of it, from which he removed various objects now lost and, as John Aubrey later thought, caused one of the stones (stone 56) to tilt over 'by being underdigged'. After this unpromising start the King approached the Royal Surveyor, Inigo Jones, and asked him to produce a report. Jones's *Stone-Heng Restored* appeared posthumously in 1655. It was the first book entirely devoted to the subject and it argued that Stonehenge was Roman. Since Jones was an architect, the discussion of his theory belongs to the next chapter, but it belongs here too because the reaction that it provoked kick-started the anti-quarian investigation of Stonehenge. If there was anything the typical antiquary liked more than proving himself right, it was proving somebody else wrong, and Jones's book prompted two people, Walter Charleton and his friend John Aubrey, to throw their energies into discrediting it.

The archaeologist Jacquetta Hawkes famously remarked that every age 'has the Stonehenge it deserves – or desires' and the Stonehenge of the Stuart antiquaries was born of the age that saw the foundation of the Royal Society, the wider exploration of the Americas and a new Baconian spirit of critical enquiry, in which nature and mathematics were the ultimate authorities. This critical, analytical cast of mind brought about a change in attitudes to the past and to the study of it. Until then history had been narrated, chiefly, as the story of a Golden Age, with everything since a long-protracted fall. 'Till about the yeare 1649,' as Aubrey noted, ''twas held a strange presumption for a man to attempt an innovation in learning; and not to be good manners to be more knowing than his neighbours and forefathers.' Enquiry now was all the rage, but it was tinged also with melancholy and foreboding. The generation of antiquaries that had lived through the Civil Wars had seen towns and families divided. They had watched Puritans smash stained glass and knock the heads off the statues in churches; they feared for the past and for the future. Charleton, who was the first to respond to Inigo Jones, had been particularly close to these events as physician to Charles I and later to his son in exile. His book, *Chorea Gigantum Or, The Most Famous Antiquity of Great Britain, Vulgarly called Stone-heng*, was published in 1663. When Charleton looked at the monument he saw the stones 'sleeping in deep Forgetfulness, and well-nigh disanimated by the Lethargy of Time'. But he also saw the spot where Charles II, now restored as king, had paused on his flight after the Battle of Worcester at one of the most desperate moments of his life. Both images haunt Charleton's treatise and inform its surprising conclusion that the circle was the work of the Danes.

The argument was based on some, admittedly rather loose, comparisons with the stone circles of Denmark documented by his Danish friend and fellow antiquary Ole Worm, but the method was new and not naïve. In trying to understand Stonehenge in its own terms, without magic and in relation to the other similar monuments, Charleton was a pioneer. The dedicatory poem that prefaces *Chorea Gigantum* was written by John Dryden and it associates Charleton firmly with the new spirit of 'free-born Reason'. From now on the attempt to 'make *Stones* to live' was to be on a par with medicine and exploration as a proper study for the best minds. In the end Charleton's thesis found by analogy with Denmark that Stonehenge was not a temple, or the tomb of Boadicea as Edmund Bolton had suggested in 1624, but a meeting place for the election and coronation of kings. This was an especially happy conclusion given that Charleton's book was dedicated to his employer, Charles II. As Dryden put it:

These Ruins sheltred once *His* Sacred Head,
Then when from Wor'ster's fatal Field He fled…
His *Refuge* then was for a *Temple* shown:
But, *He* Restor'd, 'tis now become a *Throne*.

Charleton is usually written off as a sycophant as well as a poor scholar. Yet in so far as his book is a political statement, and there are few antiquarian texts of the seventeenth century which are not, he is no simple-minded royalist. *Chorea Gigantum* is not an endorsement of the Divine Right of Kings but of popular leaders, governing 'by the general suffrage of the assembly'. It dwells, to the point of tactlessness in the circumstances, on the fact that the Danes were republicans. Charleton's Stonehenge is an emblematic reminder to the restored monarch that he reigns only with the people's consent.

The treatise concludes somewhat smugly that 'this Opinion of mine, if it be erroneous, is yet highly plausible; having this advantage over the others … that it is not so easily to be refuted'. Charleton was wrong about that as well and he was not to rest on his laurels for long. Inigo Jones's former pupil John Webb retaliated rapidly with his *Vindication of Stone-Heng Restored*, but it was Charleton's friend and fellow antiquary Aubrey, having found that Inigo Jones's account gave him 'an edge' to explore the matter for himself, who completely discredited Charleton in the process of making the first great advance in the modern understanding of Stonehenge. Aubrey, best remembered today for his *Brief Lives*, was a remarkable man – the first English archaeologist, the first folklorist, the first person to attempt to date Gothic architecture by its style and the author of the first book on place names. Sceptical, anti-clerical and peace-loving, he belonged like Charleton to the new age, though he had a hankering too for the old beliefs he documented as they passed, lamenting that in his own day 'the divine art of Printing and Gunpowder' had 'frighted away Robin-good-fellow and the Fayries'. Aubrey made many innovations, but he laboured too under many difficulties. He was often in trouble, in debt and in a muddle, the despair of his friends, his notes lying about in heaps '2 quiers of paper + a dust basket', as he recalled on one topic alone, 'some whereof are to be valued'.

Considering Stonehenge, Aubrey found that Jones had 'not dealt fairly' with either the monument or his readers, while Charleton, despite 'a great deal of learning in a very good stile', had made a 'gross mistake' in thinking it Danish. Like Charleton, Aubrey favoured 'Comparative antiquity', but unlike Charleton, who had made his comparisons from written descriptions and drawings – there is nothing to suggest that he actually visited Stonehenge – Aubrey decided to rely on 'my own Eisight' and on observations 'writ on the *spott*'. In 1663 he 'took a review' of Stonehenge. This was a thorough plane-table survey, which gave him more accurate measurements and confirmed his worst suspicions about Jones's. Such precise measuring, obvious as it now seems, was novel. Aubrey's contemporary William Dugdale, a scrupulous antiquary in most respects, was content to describe a megalithic monument in Cumberland as 'about the diameter of the Thames from the Heralds' office'. Aubrey was not only more accurate, as a native of Wiltshire, he had the advantage of local knowledge, and his acute antiquarian eyesight had already helped him to one great discovery, which was to be critical to his analysis of Stonehenge. In January 1649, on a hunting trip, he saw Avebury and was the first person to recognise that it was not just a random collection of rocks but a stone circle, 'the greatest, most considerable & ye least ruinated of any of this kind in our British Isle'. 'No body hath taken notice of it before,' Aubrey remarked, 'though obvious enough.' It was not to be the last time that a great archaeological discovery with implications for Stonehenge would be made by simply looking with new eyes at what had always been there.

Avebury was the touchstone for Aubrey's comparative study. By analogy, 'a kind of Algebraical method', he found the series of holes at Stonehenge marking, as he thought, the site of stones now missing. This was, he noted to himself, 'a good remark' and the Aubrey Holes bear his name today. He disproved the historian William Camden's suggestion that Avebury had been a military camp by pointing out that the ditch was inside the 'rampart' and for defensive purposes it should be the other way round. He also dismissed Camden's suggestion that the Sarsen stones were not stone at all but some form of artificial cement, pointing out, again from observation, that such stones were to be seen all over the Marlborough Downs. Aubrey's interest in language and oral tradition led him to notice that local people called the monument 'Stonedge', meaning stones on their edges, which he thought a plausible derivation. On the question of how the sarsens got their name, he suggested that it came from the Anglo-Saxon '*sar-stan*' meaning 'troublesome or difficult stone', which still seems more likely than the conventional derivation from 'Saracen'. In conversations with local people, especially Mrs Mary Trotman, a particular source of 'good information', he gleaned the story of the Heel Stone, which in his day was stone 14, said to bear the mark of Merlin's foot as he ran from the Devil.

As Aubrey pondered all that he learned, the facts played on his imagination. Surveying the Marlborough Downs, he noted that the greywethers lying around might make one 'fancy it to have been the scene, where the Giants fought with huge stones against the Gods'. This ability to 'fancy' was as important to his understanding of Stonehenge as his plane table. Both are necessary in archaeology, as in any science, for while a pure fantasist can contribute nothing, neither is a pedant likely to have much insight. The balance of fact to imagination and personal experience in the study of Stonehenge has tipped wildly in both directions from time to time, but perhaps in Aubrey it was most perfectly poised. He looked to his own experience to interpret what he found, but more subtly and sensibly than Charleton. Considering the barrows around Stonehenge and remembering the Civil Wars, he decided that they must mark ritual burials rather than the graves of the Britons murdered by Hengist. After a battle, he noted, 'soldiers have something els to do' than build elaborate tombs. Jones's naming of the 'altar stone' he thought another case of over-interpretation: 'Perhaps they used no altar; for I find the middle of the monument voyed.'

Aubrey took a literally and intellectually broad view of Stonehenge, which he recorded in the first book of his *Monumenta Britannica* in 1665, including in it drawings of stone circles and monuments from all over the British Isles, some of which he visited, for others of which he relied on information from his fellow antiquaries. He went on to describe many ancient earthworks, some he thought British, others Roman, Saxon or Danish, and he drew a map showing the location of these sites in the south-west of England, demonstrating their density in the area of Malmesbury, Salisbury and the Welsh Marches and the continuity of this pattern with later towns and settlements. Within such a landscape Stonehenge still loomed large, but it no longer seemed an isolated wonder. Of its purpose, however, Aubrey remained uncertain. That it was a temple of some sort he was convinced and its alignment might be astronomical, but of this 'I can not determine,' he noted scrupulously, 'I can only suggest.' When it came to authorship, his comparative researches pointed Aubrey firmly in the direction of the early Britons. 'To wind up this Discourse' he wrote:

> *The Romans had no dominion in Ireland, or (at least not far) in Scotland. Therefore these temples are not to be supposed to be built by them: nor had the Danes Dominion in Wales … But all these monuments are of the same fashion and antique rudeness; wherefore I conclude, that they were erected by the Britons: and were Temples of the Druids.*

If modern archaeologists have found any quarrel with Aubrey it is with this almost passing reference to the Druids, which unwittingly ushered in more than three centuries of, from their point of view, nonsense. But the important part of Aubrey's conclusion was that he believed Stonehenge to be British and to belong to a period of what came to be called prehistory. This was a new idea and one that took time to be accepted. The later seventeenth century, the age of Newton, saw further into space than ever before, but it remained trapped in time, with a span of less than six thousand years allowed for the whole of history. Using the biblical accounts of the Creation and the Flood, which seemed to be the only evidence available, Archbishop James Ussher had calculated in 1654 that the world had been created on 22 October 4004 BC (which was a Saturday) and this was a generally accepted, if increasingly awkward, fact for some time to come. Aubrey, however, was a sceptic. He referred to the Bible very little in his writings and was prepared to speculate that 'the world is much older than is commonly supposed'. His collections of folk tales and local customs gave him a glimpse of a pre-Christian world, and he knew from his reading about the newly encountered inhabitants of the Americas. He was able to conceive of a time and a society that was neither recorded in writing nor yet merely mythological, within which a whole, real culture might exist and might create monuments. As for the Druids, according to the scant classical sources, they were the priests of the early Britons and Aubrey did not elaborate on them in this context, merely assuming, reasonably enough, that at that date they would have been responsible for religious rites and buildings.

In 1663 Aubrey presented a paper about Avebury to the Royal Society, the first archaeological paper ever delivered. Two years later he had completed his accounts of Avebury and Stonehenge, and King Charles, to whom Charleton, rather generously in the circumstances, had introduced him, was anxious that he should publish them. But Aubrey hated to finish anything. He went on adding to his *Monumenta Britannica* until 1693 and, despite later efforts by Aubrey himself and others to organise the material, it remained unpublished at his death in 1697. It appeared in a printed, partially edited form only in 1982. So, despite their importance, his findings had little immediate influence, certainly much less than those of Aylett Sammes, whose *Britannia Antiqua Illustrata*, came out in 1676. Sammes is a prime example of that kind of antiquarianism which is at the same time both completely wrong and highly important. Sammes was a lawyer and an antiquary. Almost nothing in his book was true, but the images he planted in his readers' imaginations were indelible. His theory was that the Phoenicians, an eastern Mediterranean

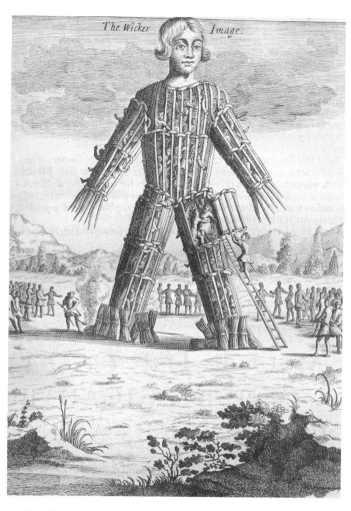

5. The Wicker Man from Aylett Sammes's *Britannia Antiqua Illustrata* of 1676. A wild extrapolation from Caesar's account of Druid sacrifices, the image inspired Wordsworth and Blake as well as the cult film of 1973.

people from Tyre, had travelled as far as Britain and become its first inhabitants. This was already a current idea, but Sammes took it to new heights, or depths, of elaboration using highly speculative etymology. 'Not only the name of Britain itself, but of most places therein of ancient denomination are purely derived from the Phoenician Tongue', he asserted, without explanation, 'the Language itself for the most part, as well as the Customs, Religions, Idols, Offices, Dignities of the Ancient Britains are all clearly Phoenician, as likewise their instruments of war.' The Phoenicians, who spoke Hebrew, had settled the coasts, he went on. The interior inhabitants, the Celts, and their priests, the Druids, were drawn into the Phoenicians' cult of Hercules, who had also come to Britain and was worshipped under the name of Ogmius at Stonehenge.

Although Sammes was described variously by contemporaries as 'an impertinent, girning and pedantical coxcomb' and 'not at all qualify'd', his *Britannia Antiqua Illustrata* got into the cultural bloodstream. It was the extraordinarily vivid pictures that did it. His images of a Druid and an ancient Briton had the persuasiveness that his text so lacked and lie behind innumerable later books, plays and even operas. But it was the picture of the wicker man, a gigantic figure – first described by Caesar in one of the few contemporary accounts of Druids – into which the sacrificial victims were tied before being burned alive, that is most powerful. It lives on in the work of Blake and Wordsworth, and nearly three hundred years later it was strange and frightening enough to be the basis of a cult film. First made in 1973, starring Edward Woodward and Christopher Lee, and remade as recently as 2006 with Nicolas Cage, *The Wicker Man* now has a place in the iconography of modern horror. Meanwhile, once looked for, Phoenician antiquities began to be discovered and went on turning up for centuries. At Margate in Kent there is an elaborately decorated shell grotto, first excavated in 1835 and looking, to the uninformed eye, like a late Georgian creation, which was found to be a Phoenician construction of about two thousand years old and was still shown to visitors as such in the 1990s.

So it was that by 1695, when Edmund Gibson's new edition of William Camden's *Britannia* was published, Gibson could complain with some justice about the imbalance of 'notions' to facts. Gibson knew Aubrey and coaxed him into preparing a manuscript for publication, but it was too unwieldy. Instead, Thomas Tanner, who undertook the Stonehenge section of *Britannia* summarised Aubrey's findings. He also worked his way through the other theories, dismissing the Phoenician idea, which 'has met with so little approbation'. In the end he decided on an explanation that was a mixture of Aubrey and Jones, concluding that the circle was a British monument, but not prehistoric, having been built in imitation of Roman architecture after the invasion. There was one person, however, who took Aubrey's Druid theory very seriously indeed. This was the philosopher and freethinker John Toland. Toland was an Irishman who had rejected, violently, the Catholicism of his childhood and established an international reputation as a Protestant scholar. He was an acquaintance of the philosopher John Locke, whose theories Toland countered in his most famous book, *Christianity not Mysterious*, published in 1695, and he was later admired by Voltaire. It was Toland who seems to have coined the word 'Pantheism' for a belief in God as 'the omnipresent space in which all material and immaterial distinctions are intelligible', a belief to which Aubrey was certainly inclined. Toland met Aubrey and found him 'a very honest man' albeit 'extremely superstitious' and 'the only person I ever met, who had a right notion of the Temples of the Druids'. This right notion, according to Toland, was that the Druids had indeed created Stonehenge and a great deal else. A brilliant linguist, familiar with Gaelic and Norse languages and their surviving literature, Toland thought he could reconstruct from the written sources the whole of Druid civilisation.

Of the original Druids contemporary descriptions are few and most of them relate to Gaul. Only Caesar and Tacitus refer to British Druids, but Caesar's remark that Druidism was British originally and that Gallic Druids went to Britain to study, allowed for much patriotic extrapolation on this side of the Channel. The only supposedly eyewitness account of British Druids in action is Tacitus's description of them on Mona (Anglesey) terrifying Roman troops with a spectacular display of cursing, after which they were all massacred. The other scant information about Druids refers to their worshipping in oak groves, cutting mistletoe and carrying out horrific human sacrifices, and it was used, very selectively, by later antiquaries. Although a modern view of prehistory makes it clear that the Druids, in so far as they are documented at all, are described at a period very much later than that of Stonehenge, there was nothing in Toland's time to suggest this. It was difficult enough to imagine a pre-Roman Britain at all, and if it had to fit into Archbishop Ussher's time-span it must have been short-lived, so Toland assumed, not unreasonably, that all his Celtic sources were contemporary with the Druids and with their temples. His 'Critical History of the Celtic Religion and Learning', an account of 'the philosophy of the

Druids concerning the Gods, human souls, Nature in general, and in particular the Heavenly Bodies', was a vivid narrative. Druids, with their short hair, long beards and magic wands, making sacrifices at midsummer, became moving figures in Aubrey's megalithic landscape, though they were not to Toland attractive. With their 'priestcraft' and their desire to keep knowledge to themselves, they 'dextrously led the people blindfold', in very much the way that Toland believed the Catholic clergy did in Ireland. But if not admirable, his 'retir'd and contemplative Druid' was compelling.

When Toland died in 1722 his work, like Aubrey's, was still unpublished. His *History of the Druids* appeared only in 1726. For the general reader unpersuaded by Sammes there was therefore a hiatus in the study of the ancient past. Pepys, who went to Stonehenge on 11 June 1668, had noted tersely of the stones, 'God know what their use was', and Daniel Defoe, touring Britain in the 1720s, was in more or less the same position as he looked at the standing stones at Bosca-wen in Cornwall with mildly irritated bafflement: 'all that can be learn'd from them is, that here they are,' he remarked, and moved on. Soon, however, there would be much more to say about ancient monuments, when the archaeological survey of Stonehenge and the history of the Druids were united in the work of one of the greatest antiquaries ever to consider the subject, William Stukeley. Stukeley is the figure who domi-nates and divides the story of antiquarian Stonehenge studies. The publication of his *Stonehenge* in 1740 was a watershed. It brought the subject into the public domain for the first time as an object of scientific study, to be measured, described and analysed, as well as making it a stop on every tourist's itiner-ary. It also established it, more controversially, as the work of the Druids and the site of elaborate proto-Christian rituals. For modern archaeologists Stukeley is a difficult figure, apparently mad, like Hamlet, north-north west. He began, they have argued, as a perfectly sensible field archaeologist who, in 1729, was ordained in the Church of England, contracted religious mania and invented a Druid civilisation to justify his insane theological views. But Stukeley cannot be neatly sliced in half. It would perhaps be truer to see him as a man whose lifetime spanned a shift of sensibility which he strove to understand and reconcile with his own, admittedly peculiar, spiritual experience.

Born in 1687, the year Newton's *Principia Mathematica* was published, Stukeley read law at Cambridge but later trained as a doctor. Like Aubrey, he had among his friends some of the most eminent men of his age, including Newton himself. It was to Stukeley that Newton told the story of watching an apple fall and how it made him consider the question of gravity. Stukeley was Newton's first biographer, a fellow of the Royal Society and the first secretary of the Society of Antiquaries. From a young age he had cultivated an interest in local antiquities. At a time when smart people took a Grand Tour of the Continent, Stukeley argued that 'a more intimate knowledge of Brittan' was of greater use and at least as interesting in educating the 'young nobility and gentry'. As early as 1719 the Royal Society was thanking him for his 'Curious Communications' on the subject of Stonehenge. 'Curious' was a term of unqualified praise in antiquarian circles and in 1724 Stukeley published his *Itinerarium Curiosum*, a tour of places of interest ranging from Hadrian's Wall to country houses. It was the sight of Aubrey's unpublished manuscript, however, which inspired him to concentrate on Stonehenge

Inward view of Stonehenge.
from the ♯ high altar.

5. A drawing from William Stukeley's manuscript. Stukeley spent many years
studying Stonehenge before producing his controversial book in 1740.

and Avebury. For five years he made regular summer visits to both sites and excavated some of the nearby barrows. He walked and rode, measured and pondered, accompanied on some of his trips by his patron, Lord Winchelsea. One day in 1723, for variety's sake, the two of them had dinner on top of one of the trilithons. Stukeley's survey of Stonehenge and its environs was not bettered for another hundred and fifty years. Like a true antiquary, he brought the skills of one discipline to bear upon another. As a doctor he is thought to have been the first anatomist to practise vertical dissection and he applied this technique to his archaeology, working carefully down through the strata and keeping detailed notes and drawings. He also took his own measurements. Like Aubrey and Charleton, he was anxious to refute Inigo Jones and he realised that if no unit of measurement at Stonehenge corresponded to the Roman foot, then he was not dealing with a Roman monument. This proved to be the case. He discovered instead a unit which he named the Druid's cubit, which was about 20^4/$_5$ English inches.

Stukeley rediscovered the Avenue at Stonehenge. It was he who named the trilithons, from the Greek for three stones, and he who observed and named the earthwork which he called the Cursus, thinking that it had been an ancient sports ground. Since he made no mention of the Aubrey Holes, it seems likely that they had by now been filled in, but he did notice what had been 'never previously observed', that the principal axis was aligned, more or less, with the midsummer sunrise. This, along with the Cursus, as Stukeley noted, 'very much enlarges the idea we ought to entertain of the magnificence and prodigious extent of the thing'. This was one of his greatest contributions to the subject, his ability to

7. Stukeley's view looking up the Avenue. He was the first person to appreciate the full extent of Stonehenge and to understand it as part of a connected landscape.

look out from Stonehenge into the surrounding landscape. What twentieth-century archaeologists came to appreciate once more as the 'complex web of intervisibility' on Salisbury Plain was obvious at once to Stukeley. It was obvious not least because he lived in the first great age of landscape gardening. The idea of shaping nature to aesthetic purpose, of placing in it features redolent with associative meaning, was thoroughly familiar to him. The Earl of Pembroke, to whom Stukeley dedicated his *Abury* of 1743, had a 'costly model of Stonehenge' in his grounds at Wilton, while Stukeley himself, more modestly, landscaped a ring of trees in his own garden at Grantham into a Druid grove. In his descriptions he talked and thought in terms of avenues, walks and prospects and at Stonehenge he found the summit of the landscape gardener's genius, a 'magnificent wonder … apt to put a thinking and judicious person into a kind of ecstasy, when he views the struggle between art and nature'. It is not putting it too strongly to say that Stukeley loved Stonehenge. His aesthetic appreciation of it was acute, intense and spiritual. He noticed that the sarsens were tooled – 'chizel'd and far from rude' – and that they were worked more finely on the inside than the out. He observed the tapering of the uprights to correct the effect of perspective, such as the Greeks had practised in architecture. His Stonehenge was 'a true master-piece. Every thing proper, bold, astonishing. The lights and shades adapted with inconceivable justness … the proportions of the dissimilar parts recommend the whole, and it pleases like a magic spell.'

Stukeley made a great contribution to the understanding of what the prehistoric Stonehenge had been. His work is still invoked by modern archaeologists. Later, in his interpretation of his findings, he gave the monument much of the popular resonance it has today and so both aspects of his study deserve serious attention.

Over the years that he considered Stonehenge, Stukeley's view of history and of the human condition changed, in a way that disconcerted some of his contemporaries and his later critics, but which is not in itself perhaps incomprehensible. His *Stonehenge*, when it finally appeared in 1740, was cast as the first volume of a projected study of *Patriarchal Christianity: or, a chronological history of the origin and progress of true Religion and of Idolatry*. A profoundly thoughtful and pious man, Stukeley had always been anxious to discover the meaning of this wonderful 'Universe of things' in which he found himself. What he sought was a single first cause: 'We must go up to the fountainhead as much as possible,' as he put it. Like Newton (whose own theory was that Stonehenge was a temple of the earliest religion), Stukeley sought a fuller explanation of existence, but not a godless one. He lived at a time when the search for such certainty was becoming more complicated and more urgent. The horizons of the European mind were expanding through exploration, faster than in Aubrey's day, and the published accounts of travels to Egypt and the Americas told of other peoples and cultures, new plants and animals, Incan temples and similar mysterious structures. It all raised questions about the biblical framework through which history and the nature of mankind were still understood. How could so many people, living and dying beyond the reach of Christianity, be simply lost to salvation? Why were the religions of Peru and China and Egypt in certain ways similar? How could so many different sorts of animals have fitted into the Ark and where, after the Flood,

A British Druid

8. The figure of the Druid as he appeared in Stukeley's *Stonehenge* of 1740.
From that date onwards the Druids were to be indelibly associated with
the monument.

did all the water go? Stukeley struggled to understand, to justify the ways of God to man and reconcile his faith with the experience of his generation. He was immensely energetic in his intellectual efforts. In 1735 he was learning Chinese.

Between his first survey and his finished book he moved from a deist position, a belief that humans have an innate moral sense and that reason, rather than revelation, is the basis of faith, to a profoundly Christian one. His Stonehenge changed with him from a Neoplatonic model of the cosmos that could transmit 'the divine influences of the archetypal mind' to a material world into a more or less Christian church, and his Druids became priests of a religion established by Abraham and 'so extremely like Christianity, that in effect, it differed from it only in this: they believed in a Messiah who was to come into the world, as we believe in him that is come'. As his unifying theory emerged, Stukeley looked for material that might support it and found plenty in the writings of John Toland and indeed in those of Aylett Sammes. As Toland had noted, people 'easily … convey their own ideas into other men's books, or find 'em there', and to some extent this is what Stukeley did. He was prepared even to allow Sammes's Herculean visit to Britain. From his reading, Stukeley described – or conjectured – the rituals that took place at Stonehenge and deduced from them complicated arguments about the Druids' intuiting of Christianity and the Trinity. This belief in a single patriarchal ur-religion that had spread across the world and reached the early Britons was by no means peculiar to Stukeley, but the particular ways in which his native Druids had anticipated the Virgin Birth and the Crucifixion were.

When the book appeared, many of Stukeley's

contemporaries were sceptical about it and even more so when his *Abury* followed three years later. Here again Stukeley offered a detailed survey and an invaluable record of the site, noting the recent destruction of parts of it by farming. But he also found Avebury to be a 'serpentine' temple, laid out like an Egyptian hieroglyph to symbolise a snake passing through a circle. In his belief that he was dealing with an allegorical landscape 'a picture', as he put it, of Druidic faith, he allowed himself to adjust the measurements he had so carefully made to fit what he believed was a higher truth. What happened in Stukeley's inner life nobody now can know. His ordination in 1729 astonished his friends and may have marked a moment of spiritual revelation, or it may merely have been one stage along his curious journey. For all that Stukeley was sincere in his profession of faith, the Anglican Church of his day was hardly a hotbed of religious enthusiasm, nor were the average clergyman's duties onerous. Like many an antiquary before and since, he may have realised that a steady income in a quiet parish would allow him time to pursue his researches. Charles Darwin, a century later, seriously contemplated the same course for the same reason.

Yet whatever the process, Stukeley found himself drawn ever deeper into his strange visions. His friend Roger Gale warned him there would be 'great carping and piqueering upon everything you advance' and so there was and is. But Stukeley's admirers were many. Domestic tourism of the sort he had always advocated was becoming increasingly popular and his descriptions were lifted wholesale for guidebooks. Later editions of Defoe's *Tour Through the Whole Island of Great Britain* were amended to include references to Stonehenge as a Druid temple and by 1750 visitors were advised to 'Take a staff 10 feet 4 inches and ¾ long, [and] divide it into six equal Parts: These', it was explained, 'are the Cubits of the Antients.' Not everyone felt the charm of Druidry. Dr Johnson, to whom Stukeley dedicated the *Itinerarium Curiosum*, was unimpressed. In his *Tour of the Hebrides* he remarked that 'to go and see one druidical temple is only to see that it is nothing, for there is neither art nor power in it; and seeing one is quite enough'. But if Johnson was bored by the Druid remains he did not question that that was what they were. By 1787 Joseph Strutt's *Chronicle of England* had a whole chapter on the Druidical religion of the Britons and that 'curious remaining proof of their indefatigable labours, Stone Henge'. Stukeley's Druid Britain lay behind Blake's Albion, it influences the New Age Druids of today and has once again been the subject of lively debate in very recent years.

After Aubrey and Stukeley no later antiquary made so great an impression on Stonehenge studies, but several made substantial contributions. William Cooke hastened into print in 1754. He sought to support Stukeley on nearly every point, especially his suggestion that the name Chorea Gigantum was a corruption by 'trifling monks' of the original '*choir gaur*', which derived from the Hebrew – via Welsh – for 'circular high place of the assembly or congregation'. After Stukeley Choir Gaur became the preferred name for the monument among those who felt they had a really original theory to offer. Dr John Smith's *Choir Gaur* of 1771 was subtitled 'The Grand Orrery of the Ancient Druids … Astronomically explained, and mathematically proved to be a TEMPLE erected … for observing the motions of the HEAVENLY BODIES'. It was Smith who launched the idea of Stonehenge as an observatory, aligned with both summer and winter solstices.

He was able to be more definite about this than Stukeley for he had one great advantage over him. In 1752 England at last adopted the Gregorian calendar. The old Julian calendar of Stukeley's day had been falling behind for centuries and Stukeley could not be sure when midsummer was. His 21 June was really 3 July. But Smith knew the date exactly and so could visualise 'the Druid in his stall' at the centre of Stonehenge, watching the sun rise over the marker to which Smith now attached the name of Heel Stone, by which it has been known ever since. In fact the sun rises just to the north of the Heel Stone, a point which has at varying times been made to count both for and against astronomical alignment. In Smith's book the outer circle represented the solar year, the inner one the lunar month. The theme was taken up again in 1846 by the Reverend Edward Duke in his *Druidical Temples of the County of Wiltshire*, which was responsible for naming the Station Stones, but it was only in the twentieth century that astronomy became a major element in the discussion of Stonehenge, rivalling the Druids as an irritant to archaeology.

Edward King's *Munimenta Antiqua* of 1799 had 'more of fanaticism than historical discrimination' in it, according to his fellow antiquary and Stonehenge enthusiast John Britton. But its lurid naming of the Slaughter Stone has stuck and it had one great event to report. On 3 January 1797 a horse pulling a cart along a road 'at a distance' from Stonehenge was startled by an almighty reverberating crash that sent a tremor through the ground. The western trilithon had fallen, its lintel breaking as it fell. It was to lie there prone for more than a century. But, as is often the case in archaeology, catastrophe was also opportunity. The upheaval of the ground and the chance to examine the underside of the uprights was welcomed by William Cunnington, a wool merchant and antiquary who lived at Heytesbury, about ten miles from Stonehenge. It was he who began the next stage of on-site investigation. In 1801 he published his 'Account of tumuli opened in Wiltshire', which attracted the notice of Sir Richard Colt Hoare, whose home was at Stourhead nearby and who sponsored Cunnington's work. From 1810 to 1812 Colt Hoare published the first volume of his *Ancient History of Wiltshire*, which included the account of Stonehenge. In it he and Cunnington set out their discoveries, including many finds from the burial mounds, and their theories in measured terms. Theirs was a work of consolidation more than innovation, although their examination of the Slaughter Stone showed it to have been worked equally on three sides, suggesting that it had once stood upright and had never been the blood-soaked site of sacrifice that King imagined.

'We speak from facts not theory,' Colt Hoare stated at the beginning of his *Ancient History*, and he and Cunnington are sometimes hailed as the founding fathers of modern British archaeology. Yet for the antiquary facts did not preclude emotional and artistic pleasure. One visitor reported, 'When Sir Richard Hoare opens tumuli, a week is generally set apart for the operations, and the Baronet … is generally attended by a party of his friends … the time passes with much festivity and good humour.' The serious work of excavation was interspersed with dinners, toasts and mock-Druidic ceremonies and if the late Georgians knew fewer facts about Stonehenge than we do, they were perhaps closer to it in their understanding of ritual and symbolic landscape. Colt Hoare's house, Stourhead, was surrounded by one of the greatest landscape gardens ever created in England. It was begun, by Henry Hoare, shortly before Stukeley published his *Abury*, and its programmatic walks, artificial mounds and structures embody that vision of landscape art and architecture which Stukeley thought he could detect on Salisbury Plain. After 1771 it included a Druid's cell built from 'old Gouty nobbly Oakes'. Cunnington (the Druid Mordred to his antiquarian intimates) had a grotto in his own garden, a modest version of the Stourhead features, with a plan of Avebury set into the floor in pebbles. While Colt Hoare had his reservations about some of Stukeley's conclusions, he shared his sense of ecstasy and concluded his own account with the observation that 'even the most indifferent passenger over the plain must be attracted by the solitary and magnificent appearance of these ruins; and all with one accord will exclaim, "HOW GRAND! HOW WONDERFUL! HOW INCOMPREHENSIBLE."'

Few travellers across the plain were indifferent by now. Those who were lucky enough to run into Cunnington himself might be treated to a sight of his museum at Heytesbury, where the finds from the barrows were on show. 'Nothing could be more curious and systematic than the arrangement of the museum,' according to one tourist at this first ever Stonehenge visitor centre. The contents of the individual burials were grouped together and interpreted to show, for example, the grave of a hunter buried with his dog: 'an epitaph could not have let us more into the rank and character of the dead,' the admiring visitor noted. This emphasis on recovering individual characters from the past was also very much of its time, a time when historical fiction and fictionalised

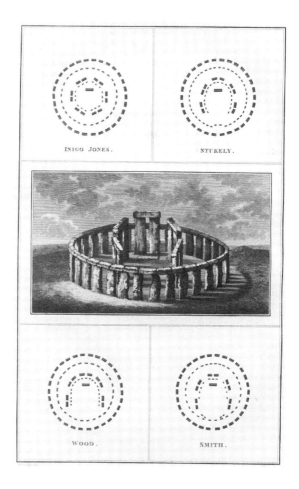

INIGO JONES.

STUKELY.

WOOD.

SMITH.

9. From William Cunnington and Richard Colt Hoare's *Ancient History of Wiltshire*, 1810–12, a plate illustrating the four most important theoretical reconstructions to date. Their book marked the beginning of modern archaeology in Britain and the effective end of antiquarian enquiry at Stonehenge.

history were becoming deeply intertwined. This was the age of Walter Scott, himself an enthusiastic antiquary, whose novels brought the past to vivid life and created an appetite for the minutiae of the Olden Times. Readers and tourists expected a good narrative with plenty of detail. Descriptions of the food, the furniture, the 'manners and customs' of bygone days were popular. In Smith and Meyrick's *Costume of the Original Inhabitants of the British Isles* of 1815, the Grand Conventional Festival of the Britons at Stonehenge is illustrated in full colour. It is a magnificent display of pageantry, a prehistoric *Ivanhoe*.

With Cunnington and Colt Hoare, however, it could be said that the antiquarian investigation of Stonehenge came, more or less, to an end. For the 'philosophical antiquary', as John Britton put it, there was no more to be done without written records. The stones remained enigmatic:

> *It would certainly be gratifying to ascertain the time of their formation – the purposes to which they were applied, – as well as the rites, ceremonies, and civil polity of the people who raised them. These may be considered the greatest desideratum of antiquarian research; but will probably ever continue such: for it is not likely that any document will be found to elucidate those points, or that such evidence will be adduced as shall be demonstrative, explicit, and unequivocal.*

Not everyone was so pessimistic or so cautious. Godfrey Higgins went into print in 1827 with an 'attempt to shew the druids were the priests of oriental colonies who emigrated from India and were … the builders of Stonehenge'. The statistician John Rickman confidently explained to the

Society of Antiquaries in 1839 that the whole structure dated from around the third century AD, with diagrams to show how it was built. But while, for the more circumspect antiquary, unequivocal evidence about Stonehenge in prehistory remained elusive, antiquarianism made considerable contributions to the historiography. As early as 1725 Thomas Hearne had published *A Fool's Bolt soon SHOTT at Stonage*, by John Gibbons, a seventeenth-century response to Inigo Jones, and the Camden Society republished the history of Polydore Vergil in 1846. Britton preserved many of Stukeley's papers and his *Memoir of John Aubrey* of 1845 brought more of Aubrey's work into print than ever before, although the manuscript of the *Monumenta Britannica* still lay, unknown to Britton, in the Bodleian Library.

Meanwhile, as antiquarianism, romanticism and then the works of Walter Scott all encouraged a more colourful and engaged relationship with the past, Stukeley's Druids began to escape from the pages of *Stonehenge* and to manifest in the outside world. In 1781 at the Kings Arms public house in Poland Street, London, Henry Hurle was inspired to found the Ancient Order of Druids, a Freemason-like body from which the modern Order of Bards, Ovates and Druids is indirectly descended. Then, on 23 September 1792, the *Gentleman's Magazine* reported the first 'revived' assembly or Gorsedd of Bards, which met for the autumn equinox in a modestly improvised stone circle, on Primrose Hill. Bards, whom Toland had mentioned more or less in passing as 'another order of learned men' contemporary with the Druids and 'not yet quite extinct' in Wales and the Highlands, had also begun to take on a life of their own and would from now on be permanently embedded with the Druids. If the Welsh

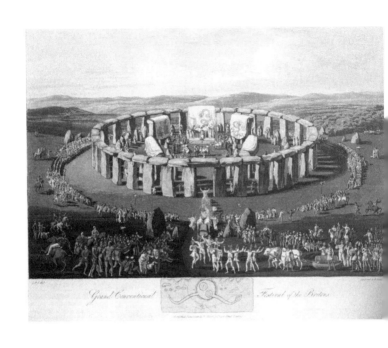

10. The 'Grand Conventional Festival of the Britons' from *Costumes of the Original Inhabitants of the British Isles*, by Samuel Rush Meyrick and Charles Hamilton Smith, 1815. This was pre-history as imagined by readers of Walter Scott.

bardic tradition had been largely mythical and moribund until the eighteenth century, by the turn of the nineteenth it too had become fact, brought into reality, of a sort, by Edward Williams. Williams, better known by the name he adopted, Iolo Morganwg, was a gifted Welsh-language poet, a forger of early Welsh literature and an enthusiastic laudanum addict whom we shall meet again. Several of his forgeries had a surprisingly long life as historic documents and another of his inventions which still survives is the Gorsedd of Bards. It began with his celebration on Primrose Hill, was taken up later in Wales and, from an initial meeting in the Ivy Bush Tavern in Carmarthen in 1819, it grew into the present-day literary and musical association, with its three ranks of Ovates, Bards and Druids – derived from Caesar. The Gorsedd and its stone circle have become an integral part of the annual Eisteddfod, the Welsh festival of literature and music, which is now the largest of its kind in Europe.

The year that the first Gorsedd met the French Revolutionary wars broke out. For most of the next twenty-three years the Continent was closed and, unable to take a Grand Tour even if they wanted to, the British turned their eyes to their native landscape and its antiquities in search of the Romantic and the Picturesque. Guidebooks, topographical prints and antiquarian literature of all sorts proliferated. Toland's *History of the Druids* was reprinted.

By the middle of the nineteenth century Stonehenge and Druidry were indissolubly linked in the mind of every cultivated person. Two hundred years of antiquarian enquiry had transformed the monument. The antiquaries of the seventeenth century had found it a mystery and derelict, 'well nigh disanimated by time'. They woke it from its sleep of long

forgetfulness and left it still a mystery but animated, populated, central to the understanding of Britain's earliest history
and to its cultural imagination. In short, they made it what
it is today.

3

ART, ORDER AND PROPORTION:
THE ARCHITECTS

'I saw Stonehenge today – the soul of architecture laid bare.'
John Summerson in a letter to Gavin Stamp, 1982

Whatever else it may or may not be, Stonehenge is certainly architecture. It is a building aesthetically conceived. The sarsens are more elaborately worked on the inner than the outer face. The lintels curve, following the circle of the uprights, and the trilithons rise in height towards the middle. It may be, too, as Stukeley and others have thought, that the uprights taper to compensate for the effects of perspective. Inside and outside, symmetry and centrality, these are architectural ideas, and if Stukeley was the most lyrical admirer of Stonehenge as art, Inigo Jones was its first apologist. He began his treatise with a eulogy to a building 'different in Form from all I had seen before'; 'likewise of as beautiful Proportions, as elegant in Order and as stately in Aspect, as any'. Yet despite the fact that his *Stone-Heng Restored* was the first book published on the subject and the one that gave the Altar Stone its name, Jones, like John Wood, author of the other principal architectural account of Stonehenge, has had a poor press. He has been accused since Charleton and

Aubrey's day of bending the monument to fit his theories and his treatise has in recent years been dismissed as 'valueless', 'phoney', 'tiresome' and 'a travesty'. This is to judge it by the wrong criteria. Jones and Wood, although they did undertake measurements and suggest dates, were not antiquaries or archaeologists. They were architects and they sought to place Stonehenge in the history of architecture. They undoubtedly used it as a magnifying glass to enlarge their own artistic ideas, but in so doing they carried it with them from the past into the future. Both men in their day revolutionised town planning. Between them they transformed the streets of London, Bath and indirectly many other towns and cities. Thanks to them, a vision of Stonehenge is built into the urban fabric of modern Britain.

Inigo Jones's was by far the more impressive career. It was he who brought the Italian Renaissance to British architecture and thereby 'determined the course of … almost three centuries'. He also designed the Banqueting House in Whitehall for Charles I. Despite which, many gaps remain in our knowledge of him. He was born in London in 1573, the son of a joiner, also called Inigo. Why the Jones family favoured this exotic Spanish Christian name, and indeed what happened in the first thirty or so years of the younger Inigo's life, remain obscure. He began his career as a joiner like his father before, travelling in 'the politer Parts of Europe', Italy, France and possibly Denmark. Italian architecture made a deep impression on him. He became fluent in the language and brought back the most important architectural texts of the Renaissance, the works of the Roman architectural theorist Vitruvius, Palladio's *Quattro Libri dell'Architettura* and many others. His friend the antiquary Edmund Bolton, author of the Boadicea-Stonehenge theory, was hopeful that through Jones 'sculpture, modelling, architecture, painting, acting, and all that is praiseworthy in the arts of the ancients will soon find their way across the Alps into our England'. Jones didn't manage quite so much, but he did make a transforming contribution first to British theatre, as a designer of masques, and later to architecture.

How such a sophisticated man, who had seen the Colosseum for himself, could have thought that Stonehenge was an example of Roman architecture is something that has puzzled many people since 1655, when *Stone-Heng Restored* was published. Described by the architectural historian John Summerson as an intelligent book with a ludicrous conclusion, *Stone-Heng* is most profitably read as a glimpse into the mind of a great architect at a critical moment in architectural history. In its pages we see Jones revolving his thoughts about his art and its meaning at a time when to think in such terms at all was in itself original. Jones was not only the first English classical architect, he was largely responsible for creating the very concept of 'architecture', a word hardly used in his lifetime. Buildings, which had changed in detail but not much in fundamentals since the Middle Ages, were put up by builders and surveyors. When, in 1615, Jones became in effect the royal architect, his title was Surveyor of the King's Works. Decades later it was still the case, as his pupil John Webb indignantly complained in his *Vindication* of Jones's *Stone-Heng*, that 'some English Monsieurs' thought of architecture merely as 'a mechanick art and unfit for Gentlemen'. In the process of dignifying Stonehenge, Jones's treatise was seeking to dignify architecture itself, placing it among the arts, high above the lowly world of trade. This of course meant elevating the architect as well. He must be a scholar and a gentleman, as described by Vitruvius: 'perfect in Design, expert in Geometry, well seen in the Opticks, skilful in Arithmetick, a good Historian, a diligent hearer of Philosophers, well experienc'd in Physick, Musick, Law and Astrology'. When Jones looked for the creators of Stonehenge, he was looking for a civilisation that could produce such men. This enabled him to dismiss the Druids, for he was familiar with the classical texts and he knew that they contained 'no mention' that Druids 'were at any Time either studious in Architecture … or skilful in any thing else conducing thereunto'. In fact the only civilisation Jones could imagine giving rise to serious architecture was Rome. The argument, like the monument, was circular, the conclusion implicit in the conception. Nevertheless, en route to his inevitable verdict Jones did invoke some of the facts, chiefly that no Roman writers mentioned Stonehenge, which persuaded him, easily enough, that 'there was no such thing in Britain, before the Romans arrived here'.

When it came to Stonehenge itself Jones sought to understand it first through its 'beautiful Proportions'. Proportion was the defining characteristic of Vitruvian architecture, in which the diameter of the column was the basic module. By multiplying or dividing it, structures of perfect design and pure mathematical clarity could be achieved. In his own work Jones became obsessed with proportion, believing that through it architecture could combine the measurable with the metaphysical. The ideal Vitruvian architect, as he noted, was as well versed in Astrology as in Arithmetick and a strong vein of mysticism ran through the Renaissance Neoplatonism that Jones, like Stukeley in his pre-Druid days, espoused. He believed in sacred geometry, a proportional system that reflected the Platonic ideal, the underlying harmony of the universe, a geometry that might indeed do more than reflect it, might actually reanimate it. The idea was not peculiar to Jones. Mathematics and mechanics, or 'menadrie', were closely allied with magic in the works of such Elizabethan scholars as the celebrated Dr Dee and although Dee was long dead he was an influence on Jones. He had written about Vitruvius before Jones was born and his Preface to *Euclid's Geometrie* is quoted in *Stone-Heng*. Overall the book expresses the sensibility of a mind on the brink of modern science, belonging intellectually to both the old world and the new. On the one hand Jones had no hesitation in finding Geoffrey of Monmouth's Merlin story 'meerly fabulous', not least because he knew from professional experience that large stones can be lifted by engineers, that obelisks had been moved by the Romans, as easily as 'to raise a May-pole'. He was similarly dismissive of Camden's suggestion that the sarsens were made of cement, pointing out that the stone occurred naturally on the Marlborough Downs. At the same time there linger in *Stone-Heng*, as in Aubrey's writings, echoes of the old magical interpretation of the world and it is in fact these, rather than the points on which Jones is, by modern lights, 'right', that give his treatise its interest and its importance.

Jones's own design for Charles I's great palace at Whitehall, though it was never built, was based on theories of sacred geometry and the supposed dimensions of Solomon's Temple. A triangle placed on the ground plan had its apex on the altar of the Chapel Royal, the whole design fitted exactly into a circle. When he came to measure Stonehenge, Jones was looking for a key that would unlock its meaning as the triangles and circles explained his Whitehall. 'Nothing more argues the ingenuity and acuteness of an Architect,' Webb wrote in his *Vindication*, 'than the accommodating of what he hath seen, or read, into the Subject whereof he is to treat and the occasion he hath in hand.' Jones used a great deal of ingenuity to find what he was looking for on Salisbury Plain – ingenuity, but not dishonesty. Architects often draw buildings, their own and other people's, not as they are, misshapen by time, marred by design faults, construction errors and lack of money, but as they ought to be. Jones found that the ideal, Platonic, Stonehenge was in the form of a central hexagon of trilithons surrounded by a double circular 'portico'. The hexagon, like the circle, was one of the perfect centralised forms favoured by Renaissance architects. The ground plan, thus revealed, consisted of 'four equilateral Triangles, inscribed within the Circumference of a circle… an Architectonical Scheme used by the Romans'. This could be divided by equilateral triangles into twelve sections, 'such as the Astrologers use in describing the twelve celestial Signs in musical Proportions'. From this, Jones realised, he had discovered a temple to Coelus, the god of the heavens, 'whom Antiquity reputed the very Stem whence all those Deities in succeeding Ages proceeded'.

However, when it came to finding an authoritative precedent for this very unusual Roman temple, Jones could only produce one model from Vitruvius and this, as critics swiftly pointed out, was a plan not for a temple but for a theatre. Here too it seems possible that Jones was not merely fudging, but accommodating his evidence to what he believed to be larger ideas. Perhaps he was thinking not only of Vitruvius but also of his contemporary Robert Fludd. Fludd had invented a memory theatre, an elaborate, semi-mystical mnemonic system which he published in 1617 and dedicated to James I. This theatre, which purported to contain all the knowledge of the greater and lesser worlds of creation, was a diagrammatic building, based on a real theatre, possibly Shakespeare's Globe. As a theatre designer himself, Jones may have been struck by the potential of the form for sacred and mystical rather than merely mnemonic purposes.

But perhaps the most intelligent aspect of Jones's ludicrous conclusion was his suggestion that Stonehenge was not merely Roman but specifically a building in the Tuscan style, the most primitive and rustic of the classical orders. Here too he had his reasons. As well as being mathematically pure and culturally important, architecture, for the official architect of the Stuart court, must also be patriotic. When Jones's employer, James VI of Scotland, ascended to the English throne in 1603 he had united, in name at least, the two nations. In 1604 James proclaimed himself monarch of Great Britain, a single Protestant kingdom, uneasily perched off the shore of a hostile Catholic Europe. It was an ideal easier to describe than to achieve. The very next year a search of the cellars of the Palace of Westminster discovered Guy Fawkes and thirty-five barrels of gunpowder. In a doomed but interesting attempt to win English sympathy, Fawkes later claimed that the reason he wanted to kill James was not because he was a Protestant, but because he was Scottish. At home, as much as abroad, the vision of Britannia Triumphans was a matter of physical and dynastic survival for the Stuarts. It loomed large in the iconography of James and Charles I, and nowhere larger than in Rubens's great ceiling paintings in Jones's Whitehall Banqueting House. This, the 'greatest baroque ceiling north of the Alps', presents a complex allegorical scheme probably devised, at least in part, by Jones. In it James I and VI appears as the new Solomon, seated in a circular temple whose form symbolises concord. Britannia, we now see, as the imagery unfolds, is not at all a new idea dating merely from 1603, it is the revival of the ancient, original faith and national identity of these islands. This identity is of course Protestant and traces its descent back to a hazy dawn in which the foundation myth of the Trojan Brut, the story of Joseph of Arimathea's visit to England and the sacred geometry of Solomon's Temple all play important, if ill-defined parts.

In forming his conclusion that Stonehenge was Tuscan, Jones adopted the same approach. As James sought to promote Britannia, so Jones urged the cause of architecture, and there is no better way to establish a new idea in a culture than by asserting its extreme antiquity. Jones advanced his architectural vision by giving it a foundation myth. Not only was Stonehenge dedicated to the sun god, the most ancient 'Stem' of all religions, it was built in this most primitive – and at first sight unlikely – of the classical orders. By the time he came to make his notes for *Stone-Heng*, Jones had thought deeply about the implications of the Tuscan, Italy's own native style. It was '… a plain, grave and humble manner of Building, very solid and strong' that represented for him a kind of ur-architecture, the 'first face of Antiquity'. In finding that 'betwixt this Island of Great Britain, and Rome it self there's no one Structure to be seen, wherein more clearly shines those harmoniacal Proportions of which only the best times could vaunt, than in this of Stone-Heng', Jones made Britain the direct heir of Rome and gave modern architecture the blessing of the ancients. It wasn't a very rigorous argument, any more than Rubens's paintings were rigorous. This was allegory, not logic. Even so, to give such importance to the question of style was as original as the discussion of architecture itself. If architecture was more than mere building, if it developed, as Vitruvius suggested, over time, then it must be possible to date it by its appearance. 'Who, that hath right Judgment in Architecture' Jones wrote in *Stone-Heng*, 'knows not the Difference, and by the Manner of their Works how to distinguish Aegyptian, Greek, and Roman Structures of old, also Italian, French and Dutch Buildings in these modern Times? Who did not by the very Order of the Work, assure himself, the Body of the Church of St Paul London, from its Tower to the West End, anciently built by the Saxons: as the Quire thereof, from the said Tower to the East End by the Normans, it being Gothick work.' Jones's critical admirer Aubrey, in some of his unpublished notes, himself made an attempt to discriminate and date the various styles of 'Gothick'. In this use of style to compare, differentiate and date buildings both men were pioneers.

To be sure, Jones's *Stone-Heng* tells us chiefly about Jones, but his architecture may in turn tell us something about Stonehenge, for the Tuscan gave him a theme as well as an origin myth. According to Vitruvius, this simple style, with its plain, robust columns was a rustic form, calling for deep, sheltering eaves. Palladio had drawn out, as a more or less theoretical exercise, an illustration showing unmoulded beams and huge projecting cantilevers. It was never meant to be used as a design, but Jones took it up in one of his most influential works, the church and piazza at Covent Garden in London. This was not a royal commission. Jones was working for Francis Russell, the Earl of Bedford, who was developing

11. Inigo Jones's piazza and the church of St Paul, Covent Garden, by Wenceslaus Hollar, *c.*1658. The scheme was a complete revolution in street planning and made use of the Tuscan style, the most primitive of the classical orders, in which Jones believed Stonehenge itself was built.

his London estate. The scheme Jones devised was for a square with terraces of identical houses over an arcaded walk with a church at one end. An open square like this was revolutionary. It had sources on the Continent, but there had been nothing like it in Britain. In London, where the crockets and spires of Gothic churches rose among timber-framed houses and inns, leaning higgledy-piggledy over the winding streets, this wide, symmetrical space with regular façades spoke dramatically of the order and proportion that Jones so admired. These houses were the first examples of what became the Georgian terrace.

The church, however, posed a challenge, both symbolic and practical. St Paul's Covent Garden was the first Protestant church to be built on a wholly new site since the Reformation. It had, in its form and its style, to proclaim the British faith, a faith as true and as old as that of Rome, but quite independent of it. It couldn't be Gothic, for Gothic had been associated since the Reformation with Catholicism. It was also, from Jones's point of view as an architect, hopelessly out of date. Then there was the practical aspect of the problem, which was money. As Webb pointed out in his *Vindication*, lay people often fail to take into account 'how Architects are compell'd to struggle with Necessity, through want of fitting Materials; and divers the like Accidents'. The necessity that had to be struggled with in this case was the Earl of Bedford's reluctance to pay very much. He had had to obtain special permission to build on the site at all and had only included a church for the purposes of what would now be called planning gain, so he wanted it to be as cheap as possible. Jones made a virtue of necessity and solved both problems at once by choosing for St Paul's, and indeed for the whole scheme, the rustic Tuscan, a style both more ancient and more novel than any other. He determined to build 'the handsomest barn in England' and with the massive portico of St Paul's Covent Garden set this most primitive form of architecture at the heart of the most sophisticated piece of town planning of its day. Francesco Milizia, the eighteenth-century critic, described the result as unique in the whole of European architecture.

According to Webb, it was not until about 1637 that Jones began to think seriously about James I's suggestion that he should produce an account of Stonehenge. By then James was dead. Jones had built Covent Garden and was working for Charles I on designs for the great palace at Whitehall, intended to outshine Philip II's Escorial. He was an architect at the height of his powers and a personality no doubt of what Summerson described as 'alarming force', a man at the forefront of national life confident to a fault of his own judgement. His Stonehenge is a microcosm of all that he now believed about architecture, its nature and its origins. How long he worked at his notes is not known. When the Civil Wars began in 1642 there came an end to his royal surveyorship, as to much else. The image of Britannia and her united kingdom was shattered. Jones was taken prisoner by the Parliamentary forces in 1645, but survived the war unscathed and lived out the rest of his life quietly in London. At his death in 1652 he left his substantial property to his pupil John Webb, who had married a relative of his master. When Webb came to publish *Stone-Heng* three years later he said that he had 'moulded off and cast into a rude Form' the 'few Indigested notes' that Jones had left. The work did not, to put it mildly, 'give a general satisfaction'. Few beyond Jones's immediate acquaintance took his conclusions seriously and as far as the investigation of Stonehenge itself was concerned the book's chief result was to spur Charleton and Aubrey on to contradict it. In architectural history, however, where Jones had most wanted to place Stonehenge, he succeeded rather better. Johann Bernhard Fischer von Erlach's *Entwurff Einer historischen Architectur* (*An Outline History of Architecture*), published in Vienna in 1721, included Stonehenge in its first volume along with the Seven Wonders of the World. It would perhaps have been an unlikely inclusion without Jones's endorsement. As late as 1817 Sir John Soane, who had a particular fascination with Stonehenge and had had his own, accurate measurements taken, was nevertheless still using Inigo Jones's plan in his lectures at the Royal Academy. And in 1958, when the architects James Stirling and James Gowan were working on a scheme for the new Churchill College, Cambridge, they conceived the design, Gowan recalled, 'in terms of something like Stonehenge'. Faced with an open expanse of land and no surrounding buildings, they were at first baffled. 'What do you do?' as Gowan put it. 'There is one thing: you can take out your compasses and cut a piece of Platonic geometry into the site.' Three hundred years after Inigo Jones, an architect looking at Stonehenge still saw Platonic geometry.

Beyond the world of architecture, however, even readers who admired Jones's work could not swallow his argument, and got around their embarrassment by suggesting the book was really written by Webb. This seems unlikely. Webb was too loyal an admirer of his master to have distorted his intentions and, to judge by his *Vindication*, far too dull and chaotic a writer to have produced all of *Stone-Heng*, which is well organised and well written. No doubt he added the antiquarian details for which his master had had less patience, but the treatise in essence is surely Jones's. Perhaps its most perceptive reader was William Stukeley. Stukeley was one of those who thought too highly of Jones to believe that he had written *Stone-Heng* and directed his considerable irritation with the obviously inaccurate plan (which must certainly be Jones's) towards Webb. Yet Stukeley, whose own response to Stonehenge was so deeply aesthetic, could see the connection between *Stone-Heng* and Jones's architecture. The 'walk', as he described it between the outer circles on Jones's plan reminded Stukeley of the 'fine circular portico, which is one great beauty among many, in [Jones's] drawings for Whitehall', while the Barber Surgeons' Hall, another of Jones's buildings in the Tuscan style, long since demolished, was similar in proportions to what Stukeley called the 'adytum', or inner sanctum, the area within the trilithons. He felt very differently about the next architect to write about Stonehenge. John Wood's *Choir Gaure* appeared in 1747, seven years after Stukeley's own *Stonehenge*. Stukeley was horrified. These 'whimsys of his own crackt imagination', these 'wild extravangancys', were intolerable and where Wood was not insanely inventive he was a plagiarist. 'The very best things in his book he has pillaged from me,' Stukeley complained, 'even the word trilithon', and he was glad to be reassured by Roger Gale that he had 'nothing to fear … it is a silly pack of stuff'. That was not quite true. Stukeley protested too much. Privately he re-read Wood's work, for the two men had certain things in common.

Born in Bath in 1704, the son of a builder, John Wood lived in an age in which architecture was widely accepted as a polite art and Britain, after the Act of Union in 1707, was a legally established entity. Yet many of the questions that interested Jones, about national and architectural origins, the compatibility, or otherwise, of Christian and classical pasts and the meaning of buildings, still hung in the air and although Jones had been dead for more than half a century, his influence was everywhere. The first volume of Colen Campbell's *Vitruvius Britannicus* appeared in 1715, establishing Jones and Palladio as the two great models for English architecture. The neo-Palladian was the architectural gospel of Wood's day and Jones was its prophet. When it came to Stonehenge, however, Wood's attitude to his hero was mixed. Like most people, he could not accept Jones's conclusions and when he surveyed the site for himself he realised that Jones's plan was wildly inaccurate. Wood's *Choir Gaure …Described, Restored and Explained* can nevertheless be seen as a kind of sequel to *Stone-Heng*, taking up the themes of sacred geometry, ancient history and symbolism as they appeared in the Hanoverian age, as classicism became tinged with the first intimations of a Romantic sensibility.

Wood's plan was the most accurate to date and is still useful to archaeologists. Despite this, however, he has been largely dismissed as an obsessive and a fantasist. Unlike Jones, Wood was a prolific author. It is not difficult to know what he thought, though why he thought it is more complicated. Like Stukeley, he believed Stonehenge and the other stone circles in the south-west of England were the works of the Druids. He, too, had read John Toland and been convinced by him. He had also read Stukeley and been less impressed. Wood may have had personal reasons for disliking Stukeley, which we shall come to later, but more importantly he had his own theory to propound. This was, put simply, a vast extrapolation from Caesar's passing reference to Britain as the centre of Druidic learning. This hint expanded in Wood's mind into a whole civilisation in which the British Druids 'had not only publick edifices for the exercise of their religion and learning; but such as were truly magnificent'. The secrets of the Druid priesthood, which Caesar says were never written down, must therefore be 'locked up', 'emblematically', in their temples.

The stone circle at Stanton Drew, eight miles south of Bristol, was, Wood found, a temple to the moon, representing 'almost all those Bodies that compose the Planetary World'. It was also, he explained, a Druid university. The philosopher Druids met at Avebury and the priests, who initiated their disciples at Okey Hole (a variant spelling of Wookey Hole), 'performed the offices assigned to their orders' at Stonehenge, which was a temple to sun and moon. Wood unrolled a vivid canvas before his readers, a landscape peopled with figures from the writings of Toland and Aylett Sammes, whom he, like Stukeley, found it convenient to take reasonably seriously. Here at the centre of proceedings is the Druid priest 'array'd in sacred robes, – his Egg about his Neck', participating in the 'mistletoe solemnity'. There is Hercules in the guise of Ogmius, who, Wood thinks it 'extremely probable', helpfully transported the greywether stones from the Marlborough Downs. In among them are some older aspects of the Stonehenge tradition. There is a surviving echo of Jones's Neoplatonism, 'what the Antients called the harmony of the Spheres', which Wood thinks is reflected in the arrangement of the stones. There is Joseph of Arimathea, who came to Glastonbury 'in the very heart of all the Druidical Works' and there is the Renaissance heliocentric universe, which the Druids understood, until their learning was suppressed by St Augustine.

Reading *Choir Gaure*, it is tempting to think that Wood is making it up as he goes along, but this is not quite true. His study of Stonehenge was only one part of a greater overarching system or 'superstructure' of beliefs which he had already set out in an earlier book, *The Origin of Building*, published in 1741. His purpose in all his work was 'to make the Account [of architectural history] consistent with Sacred History, with the confession of the Ancients and with the course of great Events in all parts of the world, and with itself'. He was looking, like Jones and to some extent Stukeley, for an architectural equivalent of the unified-field theory and he found it in the existing argument that all classical architecture was derived, or 'plagiarised' as he put it, from the design of the Tabernacle and the Temple of Solomon, designs handed down by God to the Jews. Architecture had not developed, as the pagan Vitruvius said, it was revealed fully formed to Moses.

The work that underpinned his *Origin of Building*, and indeed much of the eighteenth century's conception of pre-history, was Isaac Newton's *Chronology of Ancient Kingdoms Amended*, published in 1728. Newton, Stukeley's friend, whose character as the founding father of modern physics is so oddly shot through, to the modern mind, with mysticism, casts a long shadow over Stonehenge. His number theory, his study of the Hebrew cubit, his belief that buildings were symbolic and that the Temple of Solomon, as he hypothetically reconstructed it, was 'a hieroglyph of Jewish history' all gave a solid, scholarly impetus to Wood's own meditations and were no doubt one reason why Stukeley was so enraged by him, and yet so unable to forget him. The Temple of Solomon, as a primary source for all architecture, had been invoked in Jones's day. It was implicit in his Whitehall designs and in Rubens's ceiling. But the next century was more literal and more empirical. Newton and Stukeley both drew plans of what they believed the original temple to have been and in 1724 and 1725 wooden models were exhibited in London. In the same way the identification of the British monarch with Solomon, which had been a graceful allusion to a dead king in the ceiling at Whitehall, was also brought closer to reality in 1727 at the coronation of George II. The anthem composed by Handel for the occasion and sung at every coronation since, 'Zadok the Priest', makes it explicit: 'And Zadok the priest and Nathan the prophet anointed Solomon King.' Wood's *Origins* and the extrapolations of his *Choir Gaure* are not then so absolutely strange. In Hanoverian Britain the identification of the king with Solomon extended to the identification of the whole nation with Israel, a chosen people menaced by the Assyrians in the guise of the French, the Jacobites or any other current foe. It was a popular theme in sermons long before Blake's vision of Jerusalem 'in England's green and pleasant land'. Wood naturally rejected the name 'Stonehenge' in favour of the older, supposedly native Choir Gaur. He also calculated the Jewish cubit and, having made his survey of Stonehenge, found it, happily, to be the unit of measurement.

Of all the currents of thought that ran through Wood's writings directly into his architecture, the most powerful was his intense devotion to his birthplace, the ancient spa town of Bath. There is no more telling proof of his admiration for Inigo Jones than his recounting of the local story that Jones's mother was a native of Bath. When dealing with Geoffrey of Monmouth's account of Stonehenge, 'how ridiculous soever it may appear', Wood could not but feel there must be some truth in the idea that the stones had been a spa, used for therapeutic mineral bathing. By the same token, if Wood had a personal reason for disliking Stukeley, it may have been that in his *Itinerarium Curiosum* of 1724 Stukeley cast aspersions on the city as 'a disgrace to the architects they have there' and also on the story of the local king, Bladud, and the 'silly account of his finding out these springs, more reasonably attributed to the Romans'. Wood's builder father was one of those implicitly castigated in these remarks and Bladud was one of Wood's favourite historical characters, the key to his whole interpretation of Druid history. Wood's stinging aside on the inaccuracy of Stukeley's own survey of Stonehenge, that it was partly due to his having employed one 'Abraham Sturges a jobing [*sic*] Bricklayer and mason of Amesbury, whom he stiles an Architect', has an unmistakably personal tone. Second only, perhaps, to Jerusalem, Bath was, to Wood, the celestial city. It was, however, as Stukeley said, generally thought to be Roman, a difficulty Wood overcame by discovering in its streets a more ancient groundplan dating from the time of Bladud, an ankh within a hexagon, 'the Hieroglyphical Figure of the Antients'.

As an architect Wood wanted more than anything to build in Bath. In architecture the flights of imagination frowned on among antiquaries and historians are of the essence. He created, out of his visionary reading of Stonehenge, a scheme that was, as Summerson put it, 'unique in the urbanism of Europe', the most daring and influential thing that had been done since Inigo Jones's Covent Garden. Bath as it was in Wood's childhood had possibly deserved Stukeley's strictures. It was a provincial place, only just expanding beyond its medieval walls, where the inhabitants were said to bathe naked in

12. The Circus, Bath, designed by John Wood and begun in 1754. Wood's planning was as original as Jones's had been. The circus was a novel form that puzzled some of his contemporaries but was soon copied in London and elsewhere. Derived from Wood's study of Stonehenge, Stanton Drew and other prehistoric monuments it is crowned with Druidic acorns.

the hot springs and, periodically, deposit dead animals in them. It was the unsatisfactory nature of the accommodation in the town that led the Duke of Chandos to commission Wood's first buildings in Bath, a group of lodging houses. Soon afterwards, before he had worked out his Druid theories, Wood proposed a plan for a vastly grander development along what he thought were Roman lines. This was to comprise a royal forum, a grand circus and an imperial gymnasium. It was a scheme that had apparently little to offer Georgian England and had less to do with Roman models than Wood imagined, but it represented a daring innovation in town planning, which had still not developed in London beyond the street and the square as introduced by Jones. In 1730 Wood exhibited a design for a 'grand Circus', an amphitheatre with three roads branching out from it. It was not taken up at the time and two terraces, North and South Parade, were as far as the forum ever got. But Wood's determination to build his scheme persisted.

While he waited for other opportunities he developed Queen Square on the edge of the city, marking Bath's first step from provincial backwater to fashionable spa town. He built Gay Street, leading north from Queen Square, in the 1750s and he acquired a reputation as an architect of skill and sophistication. But he never abandoned his grand design and as he worked on his books and developed his historical ideas so the plan itself changed. Sacred geometry, the Druids and their mysteries took the place of the Romans who had first fired his imagination as a young man. When eventually the King's Circus began to be built at the top of Gay Street in the last year of Wood's life, it was, like Solomon's Temple, a hieroglyph, an encoded history of its creator. The circus as built is sixty

Hebrew cubits wide. It has thirty houses, the same number as the outer row of stones at Stonehenge, and the façades are adorned with the three sacred orders, imparted by God to the Jews and thence to Bladud – the Doric, the Ionic and the Corinthian. They are all of equal size, instead of diminishing, an idea Inigo Jones had intended for his Banqueting Hall. Crowning the King's Circus are great acorns, tributes to the Druids as 'priests of the hollow oak', while on the frieze that runs round all the houses are carved symbols: the sun, Janus, a hand grasping a sceptre, the four winds and many others.

Wood took some of them from Jones's Whitehall Palace and many from a seventeenth-century emblem book by George Wither. His most recent biographers have suggested that the whole thing was an elaborate private joke and the symbols have no serious meaning. Private it certainly was, between Wood and the Divine Architect but more than a game. Wood turned a Jacobean convention into a Romantic device. The helmeted heads and dolphins on the King's Circus proclaim a mystery while still retaining it. The meaning certainly eluded most of his contemporaries, who thought the circus looked generally Roman and specifically like the Colosseum turned inside out. 'A pretty bauble,' Smollett called it in *Humphry Clinker*, 'like Vespasian's amphitheatre turned outside in.' But however it was seen, the circus, as a piece of planning, was a new creation. Others followed in London, beginning with George Dance's St George's Circus in Southwark, then Oxford Circus, Piccadilly and more in Exeter, Edinburgh and elsewhere, until it devolved at last over time into that favourite piece of British traffic planning, the roundabout. All could trace their origins back to John Wood and through him to Stonehenge.

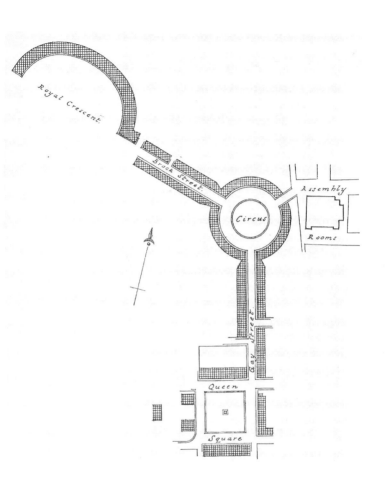

13. John Wood and his son between them created Georgian Bath in the image of a mythic past. The Circus, with its sun symbolism, was followed by the equally innovative and influential Royal Crescent, a reference to the moon.

Even more successful as an architectural form, however, was the final phase of the Wood plan, the Royal Crescent. The crescent was another new idea and one that swept Georgian Britain, was adopted by the Victorians and remains popular today. Royal Crescent was not begun until 1767, thirteen years after Wood's death. It was built by his devoted son, the younger John, who as a boy had learned the art of surveying with his father at Stonehenge. The details of the design are certainly his – they belong to a later generation – but the idea itself has its roots in Wood the elder's design. It is built in the Ionic, the order associated with the worship of the moon, and it makes a complement to the Circus, to which it is connected by Brock Street: the crescent moon of Stanton Drew to the sun of Stonehenge. For eighteenth-century Bath it was the Woods' buildings that determined both the character and the direction of its expansion, driving it northwards and uphill from Queen Square, with Gay Street pointing like the Druid arrow towards the circus and the crescent. So, while it was turning into the fashionable resort beloved of Beau Nash and loathed by Jane Austen, Bath was also becoming in fact what Wood believed it always had been, a town in whose very streets the beliefs he attributed to the early Britons can be found emblematically encoded.

Wood did not win many more adherents to his theory than Inigo Jones. His *Choir Gaure*, which deserves a modern edition, has never been reprinted. Perhaps discouraged by the fate of Wood and Jones, no major architect since has tackled Stonehenge in any detail, although it long continued to be a useful stick to beat other architects with in argument. In 1841 the Gothic Revivalist A. W. N. Pugin found, like Wood, that it offered a justification for 'The ... principle, of

Architecture resulting from religious belief'. In 'the Druidical remains of Stonehenge,' he went on, 'and in all these works of Pagan antiquity, we shall invariably find that both the plan and decoration of the building is mystical and emblematic'. Therefore by analogy, he argued, Gothic architecture, which expressed the Catholic faith, must be the truest expression of a modern Christian civilisation. Twenty-three years later the Scottish architect, Alexander 'Greek' Thomson used the same evidence to make precisely the opposite point, showing that in its posts and lintels 'Stonehenge exhibits more truthful construction than York Minster' and that therefore classical architecture was the most morally suitable for Victorian Britain.

By the 1960s, with Stonehenge firmly in the grip of archaeology and architecture in the grip of modernism, it might have seemed unlikely that there should be any more exchange between the two. But at the end of the decade, when town planning once again reached a crossroads or, it might more accurately be said, a roundabout, the influence of Stonehenge was felt again in the new town of Milton Keynes in Buckinghamshire. Milton Keynes was conceived, under the influence of the Californian sociologist Melvyn Webber, as a 'regional complex' and laid out on a loose grid to create 'urban countryside', with traffic flowing through the several zones via a succession of landscaped roundabouts. Like Covent Garden and Georgian Bath, it was a revolutionary design and the masterplan unveiled in 1969 underwent many changes as building was carried out through the 1970s. The designs were now in the hands of a group of young architects. Enthusiastic, idealistic and, by their own account, sometimes slightly drunk, they were in tune with the countercultural spirit of the age.

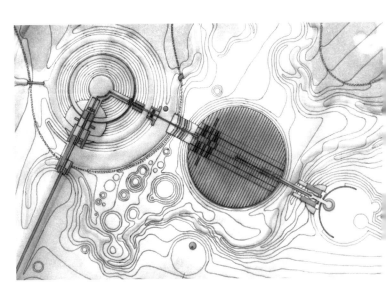

14. An unbuilt design by Andrew Mahaddie for the Central Park at Milton Keynes, 1975–6. Including a belvedere, cone and water carpet, this part of the Park was intended to continue the geometry of the centre of the town with its references to the alignments at Stonehenge.

Influenced by the writings of John Michell, whom we shall meet again later, they at one stage proposed laying out the whole town along ley lines, the mystic alignments through which, it is believed, psychic energy flows. Leys, too, will recur in the story of Stonehenge. At Milton Keynes, however, more conventional wisdom prevailed, although something of the spirit of the 1970s did make it into reality. The main streets of Milton Keynes are Avebury, Silbury and Midsummer Boulevards. They comprise a central grid which is so aligned that at the summer solstice the rising sun shines through the middle of the shopping centre, its first rays striking a large kinetic sculpture and a branch of John Lewis.

'Such as sail in the vast Ocean of Time, amongst the craggy Rocks of Antiquity', run many risks, as Inigo Jones pointed out, and it is 'far easier', as he also noted, 'to refute and contradict a false, than to set down a true and certain Resolution' in these matters. For a century or more after Wood's *Choir Gaure*, the attempts to resolve the questions raised by Stonehenge grew fewer in number as antiquarianism reached its limits. For the age of romanticism it became instead a muse, powerful in its very mystery.

4

....

'COLD STON'Y HORROR':
THE ROMANTICS

'In awful pomp & gold, in all the precious unhewn stones of Eden
They build a stupendous Building on the Plain of Salisbury ...'

William Blake, *Jerusalem*

Gradually, during the eighteenth century, the European landscape turned inside out. Civilisation was no longer found only in cities and a sympathetic interest in the natural world became a sign of 'sensibility', an increasingly popular personal quality. Partly this was a matter of taste, of that growing appreciation of landscape that infused William Stukeley's view of Stonehenge, and partly a matter of practicality. Methods of warfare had changed, making city walls and fortifications redundant. Across Britain, France and Germany ramparts came down and moats were filled in until 'towns ... [were] ... nothing but large villages' and a traveller through these open lands might think 'that universal peace had been established and the Golden Age was at hand.' So wrote Goethe in 1809, in his novel *Die Wahlverwandtschaften* (*Elective Affinities*), one of the great texts of the Romantic movement. In fact Europe, still reverberating with the aftershocks of the French Revolution, had been ravaged by war since 1792. The

15. Turner's watercolour view, engraved by Robert Wallis, 1829. The shepherd
lies dead in the storm, the sheep abandoned. For the Romantics the stones
were predominantly a place of psychic dread and terror.

physical landscape was neither tranquil nor safe and for many people, including Goethe, the interior landscape, the mental and emotional states which romanticism made the subject of art, was similarly troubled. The Stonehenge of the Romantics – primitive, enigmatic and poised somewhere between art and nature – is overwhelmingly a focus for psychic menace. It has little to do with the facts of prehistory but is much involved with those of history. If, for the Middle Ages, the stones recalled a gallows, the shadow that fell across them now was that of the guillotine.

The Romantics were not the first writers to notice Stonehenge, but previously when it figured in poetry it was usually as a symbol, standing for Britain's identity. Layamon's *Brut* or *Historia Brutonium*, written between about 1189 and 1227, was the first important poem in English after the Norman invasion, an assertion of the surviving native tradition, and it includes the Merlin story of the founding of 'Stanhenge'. For Philip Sidney, Stonehenge was one of the 'Seven Wonders of England' and for Michael Drayton, in *Poly-Olbion*, a curious long poem of 1612, it was 'best-lov'd, first wonder of the ile', yet it remained a passive thing, a 'dull heape', 'huge heapes of stones … confusde' , an enigma. It was the Romantics who animated Stonehenge, bringing it to life, as Mary Shelley's Frankenstein animated his creation, by running through it those currents of sympathy that flowed, as they believed, between the individual and the infinite.

At the height of the Romantic movement Stonehenge caught the attention of the greatest writers and artists, Wordsworth and Blake, Turner and Constable, as well as many lesser versifiers, such as the novelist Anne Radcliffe, and legions of second-rank watercolourists. By now it had become inseparable from Druidry. Long before they manifested themselves in Henry Hurle's Ancient Order of Druids in 1781, Toland and Stukeley's Druids had been seeping through from antiquarianism into art, at a time when the boundary between the two was highly permeable. In 1758 Thomas Gray's *The Bard, A Pindaric Ode* set a fashion for poems – and some paintings – that took the Druidical past as their inspiration.

If architects use facts only tangentially, then artists may dispense with them altogether or arrange them purely for effect. When antiquaries take to poetry, however, the case is altered. Their efforts tend to be viewed in a more critical light and the question of invention or deception becomes fraught. The later eighteenth century was rich in antiquarian poetry that was not quite what it seemed. The *Battle of Hastynges*, which included an account of 'Thors fam'd Temple' on 'Sarims spreddynge Playne', was not, it turned out, the work of Turgot, a tenth-century Saxon monk. It was a forgery by that quintessentially doomed Romantic youth Thomas Chatterton. In his incarnation as Iolo Morganwg, Edward Williams, the laudanum-addicted antiquary who founded the modern Gordsedd of Bards, also fabricated a quantity of poetry in the style of Dafydd ap Gwilym which went undetected for over a century. Yet Iolo objected, quite sincerely, to Gray's *Bard* on the grounds that it was historically inaccurate and confused Celtic with Scandinavian sources. Nowhere did the web of art and antiquarianism become so tangled as in the case of the Ossian poems, supposedly translations from the Gaelic by James Macpherson, which appeared in two volumes in 1765. Gray had his doubts about them and Dr Johnson declared robustly that they were 'as gross an imposition as ever the world was troubled with'. Yet Goethe admired *Ossian* and the poems impressed William Gilpin. It was Gilpin who first developed the hugely influential theory of the Picturesque, which became the aesthetic branch of romanticism.

'It is history as well as poetry,' Gilpin decided of *Ossian*, relishing Macpherson's vivid accounts of 'circles *of stones*, where our ancestors, in their nocturnal orgies, invoked the spirits which rode upon the winds'. Stonehenge itself, Gilpin decreed, was not Picturesque, in the sense that it would not compose into a satisfactory landscape painting. The stones were 'so uncouthly placed' that it was impossible to find an angle 'to form them, from any stand, into a pleasing shape'. Yet the experience of the site was powerful, belonging more to that other category of eighteenth-century aesthetic experience, popularised by Edmund Burke, the Sublime. 'It is not the *elegance of the work*, but the *grandeur of the idea*, that strikes us,' Gilpin wrote. 'The walk between the two circles … is awfully magnificent.' How much more striking it must have been, he went on, when the circle was still intact: 'To be immured, as it were, by such hideous walls of rock; and to see the landscape and the sky through such strange apertures must have thrown the imagination into a wonderful ferment.' Even so, for the Romantic traveller in search of either the Sublime or the Picturesque, Stonehenge posed a problem. It was visible from too far away and not only did this remove any element of surprise, the first sight of it made it look small and insignificant. One way round this, which was popular by the early nineteenth century and was famously deployed by William Cunnington to ensure the appropriate mental ferment, was to have the carriage blinds lowered before the party was in sight of the stones and allow them to be raised only once they were inside the circle. 'A Barrister', the author of *A Tour in Quest of Genealogy*, was one of many thus enraptured: when 'lo! We found ourselves within the area of the gigantic peristyle … the effect,' he reported, 'is wonderful.'

Gilpin and others worked out the theory of the Picturesque in great detail and contended hotly among themselves and against Burke and his idea of the Sublime, but the theoretical ins and outs mattered little to most people. 'Sublime' and 'Picturesque' were often used in the same description and Constable and Turner were not prevented by Gilpin's strictures from painting Stonehenge. What mattered was that by the late eighteenth century the association of ideas was an almost universally accepted fact. It was expected that landscape and weather would act upon the imagination and that history and poetry should feed on one another. Thus, when the young Wordsworth came to Salisbury Plain, it was not in itself surprising that he 'had a reverie and saw the past', nor that the past that rose before him owed much to Stukeley and even more to Aylett Sammes and his wicker man. Wordsworth saw:

A single Briton in his wolf-skin vest,
With shield and stone-axe, stride across the wold;
…
I called upon the darkness, and it took –
A midnight darkness seemed to come and take –
All objects from my sight; and lo, again
The desert visible by dismal flames!
It is the sacrificial altar, fed
With living men – how deep the groans! – the voice
Of those in the gigantic wicker thrills
Throughout the region far and near, pervades

> The monumental hillocks, and the pomp
> Is for both worlds, the living and the dead.

Of the various versions of the Druids and their culture available by the 1790s, the Romantics chose not Stukeley's peaceful proto-Christians but the violent priesthood of John Toland and Aylett Sammes. This dark vision on Salisbury Plain, which Wordsworth recalled in *The Prelude*, was of great importance to him. He saw it as proof of the supernatural power of the poetic gift, 'Imagination', which made the poet into a kind of prophet, 'Connected in a mighty scheme of truth' and able to perceive 'Something unseen before'. While the details of what he actually saw may seem familiar to the seasoned Stonehenge enthusiast, it was what he understood by it, the connection of 'both worlds', present and past, the immanence of the dead among the living, that enabled Wordsworth to take the material of the antiquaries and turn it into art. By the time he wrote these lines his experience on Salisbury Plain had already made the basis of two poems, the second a development of the first. In both of them the nightmare vision of ancient human sacrifice forms the background to a modern drama of cruelty and distress that has nothing to do with Druids, but is concerned instead with the great events of Wordsworth's lifetime, the French Revolution and its aftermath.

In August 1793, when Britain declared war on France, Wordsworth was on the Isle of Wight. He watched the fleet prepare to sail from Portsmouth with 'melancholy forebodings'. Not only did he sympathise with revolutionary France, he feared that the war would be 'productive of distress and misery beyond all possible calculation' for both sides,

Meanwhile, in his own country, William Pitt's government, terrified of revolution at home, was bringing in repressive measures to silence its critics, putting radicals on trial and banning anything it considered to be 'wicked and seditious writings'. The liberty on which the British prided themselves seemed to have been betrayed. Isolated in a nation gripped by anti-French fervour, Wordsworth felt himself to be 'an uninvited guest / Whom no-one own'd' in his own country. It was just weeks later, as he continued on his summer tour, that a carriage accident left him stranded near Stonehenge. There, physically and morally alone, troubled by thoughts of war and suffering, he had his vision and conceived the idea for the first poem, 'A Night on Salisbury Plain'.

It tells the story of a wanderer like the poet and his meeting with a woman who has lost her husband to the war and her children to famine and disease. The second version, 'Adventures on Salisbury Plain', was written two years later, by which time Pitt had suspended habeas corpus and poverty, hunger and unrest posed a still greater menace. In it the story of the woman is subsumed within a longer, more complex story of a sailor, discharged from the navy and left destitute, who, on his way home to his wife and children, robs and murders a stranger. In both versions Stonehenge forms the forbidding background. The 'child of darkness deep /And unknown days … Inmate of lonesome Nature's endless year' looms over the action, the manifestation of all that is cruel in human nature. The narrator of 'A Night on Salisbury Plain' flees from it in terror, but as he runs he 'often backward cast his face', for the horror that it represents is inescapable, it has come alive again in the present day. As the story unfolds, the 'spectral sights' of ancient sacrifice and battle that haunt the several wanderers on the plain find echoes in the sounds of modern warfare: 'The mine's dire earthquake, the bomb's thunder stroke' and the sickly light of 'midnight flames' from burning, looted towns. The suffering of the sailor and the woman, who, like many of their countrymen, were 'homeless near a thousand homes … And near a thousand tables pined for food', weighs modern cruelty against the savagery of the past and finds no great improvement. Reason, Wordsworth concludes, has only given us a clearer view of man's inhumanity:

> Though from huge wickers paled with circling fire
> No longer horrid shrieks and dying cries
> To ears of Daemon-Gods in peals aspire,
> To Daemon-Gods a human sacrifice;
> Though Treachery her sword no longer dyes
> In the cold blood of Truce, still, reason's ray,
> What does it more than while the tempests rise,
> With starless glooms and sounds of loud dismay,
> Reveal with still-born glimpse the terrors of our way?

Wordsworth was clearly familiar with the myths and histories surrounding Stonehenge and he drew on them as they suited his purpose, magnifying, simplifying, cutting and eliding. The whole story of Hengist's betrayal becomes a single motif, the sword of Treachery soaked in the cold blood of truce. The somewhat comical suggestion that the priests had actually stood on top of the trilithons to perform their rites becomes in Wordsworth's hands a Sublime image of 'Gigantic beings ranged in dread array' on top of 'mountains hung in air' who 'like a thousand Gods mysterious council hold'.

    William Blake made a similar but more complex use of

Druidic theories, for he was much closer to the antiquarian tradition. Blake's 'Welch Triads' of 1809 were probably inspired by Iolo's *Poems Lyrical and Pastoral*, and, as an engraver in London, Blake knew and worked for several antiquaries. His largest painting, now lost, *The Ancient Britons*, was commissioned by William Owen Pughe, an antiquary and lexicographer who collaborated with Iolo in his more respectable works and translated *Paradise Lost* into Welsh (without critical success). For Blake, history was 'the field of recurrent attempts to wake up human conscience'. He was mistrustful of official facts and not at all interested in literal authenticity. 'I Believe both Macpherson & Chatterton', he wrote, 'that what they say is Ancient is'. Blake was a mystic. While Wordsworth experienced visions that flashed upon the 'inward eye', Blake actually saw things. He saw angels on Peckham Rye and shortly before he began work on his long poem *Jerusalem* he had had a renewal of his visionary experiences and been 'again enlightened with the light I enjoyed in my youth'. He had also recently been arrested and acquitted of a charge of sedition, a charge which carried the death penalty. *Jerusalem*, like 'Adventures on Salisbury Plain', is a poem in which the ancient past speaks about modern Britain and its injustices.

The text, interwoven with Blake's drawings, covers a hundred pages through which his anger against his persecutors and against the condition of Albion, the personification of England, ricochets. 'The little villages of Middlesex & Surrey hunger and thirst … the Oppressors of Albion in every city & village / …mock at the Labourers limbs! They mock at his starved Children …', and 'Albions mountains run with blood.' In the complex iconography of Blake's apocalyptic world Stonehenge 'the cruel druid temple', forms

16. In William Blake's long poem, *Jerusalem*, Stonehenge is a powerful, brooding and almost entirely sinister presence.

part of one of many triads. It is associated with Tyburn, the place of execution at the western end of London, and with London Stone, the supposedly Roman marker to the east, from which proclamations were made and where, in 1450, the rebel Jack Cade declared himself mayor. All three are sites of violence, past, present and to come. Blake's Stonehenge, like Wordsworth's, shows the modern world haunted by history and stalked by visions, which in Blake's case presage also a millenarian future, where 'The sun was black & the moon rolld a useless globe through Britain' and 'Time was finished.' The Druids are symptomatic of the recurring decay of faith, which first wakes human consciousness and then declines into law and system, the 'natural religion' that Blake hated, for it seemed to limit both God and humanity. The forces of evil in *Jerusalem* include all rule makers and rationalists, Bacon, Voltaire and Newton, 'the great Reactor'. Its Stonehenge is:

> … a wondrous rocky World of cruel destiny
> Rocks piled on rocks reaching the stars: stretching from
>   pole to pole.
> The Building is Natural Religion & its Altars Natural
>   Morality
> A building of eternal death: whose proportions are eternal
>   despair

Blake's Stonehenge is like nothing else. Yet it is at the same time recognisable to anyone familiar with the literature. It too includes Sammes's sensational 'Wicker Idol' and also the less well-known image of Britannia from the title page of Drayton's *Poly-Olbion*. There she appears with her lovers, 'Briton Saxon Roman Norman'; Blake reverses the image and turns her into the figure of Jerusalem in an attitude of surrender, weeping against a background of trilithons. There is perhaps an echo even of Inigo Jones's *Stone-Heng* in the lines:

> … the Great Voice of the Atlantic howled over the Druid
>   Altars:
> Weeping over his Children in Stone-henge in Malden &
>   Colchester
> … What is a Church? & What
> Is a Theatre? Are they Two & not One? can they Exist
>   Separate?

But it is in the overarching idea of the poem, the belief that 'All things begin & end in Albion's Ancient Druid Rocky Shore', that Blake draws most deeply on the antiquarian tradition. He invokes the idea of Britain as the new Jerusalem, the site of the first temple. This possibility, which tantalised Inigo Jones and obsessed John Wood, came to Blake partly through Stukeley and partly through another antiquary, Jacob Bryant. 'Bryant and all antiquaries have proved', he wrote, 'All had originally one language, and one religion: this was the religion of Jesus, the everlasting Gospel. Antiquity preaches the Gospel of Jesus.' 'Was Britain the Primitive Seat of the Patriarchal Religion?' he asks in the section of *Jerusalem* addressed 'To the Jews'. 'If it is true: my title-page is also True, that Jerusalem was & is the Emanation of the Giant Albion.' For Blake this was a spiritual ideal, not a description of a literal past that could be calculated, as Wood had calculated it, by using the chronology of 'the great Reactor'. It is experienced inwardly, 'Jerusalem in every Man / A Tent & Tabernacle of Mutual Forgiveness'.

Robert Southey, who was Poet Laureate at the time *Jerusalem* was completed, thought it 'completely mad'. Blake made only one fully coloured version of the poem, noting sadly but accurately that it was 'not likely I shall get a customer for it'. Today he has many admirers, but few would claim fully to understand the involutions of his imagery. His attitude towards the Druids changed over time and Stonehenge, while it remains an evil presence throughout the poem, reappears, transfigured, on the final page. Here we see a complete stone circle with a snaking curl of trilithons on either side, a fusion of Stonehenge with Stukeley's serpent temple of Avebury. It is a positive image of restored order, of the original faith, perhaps, before its decline into law and natural religion. Given so much ambiguity, it is not surprising that there have been attempts to recruit Blake for the Druid cause. In the twentieth century the Druid Order of the Universal Bond claimed him as a forebear and his name has also been associated with a copper medal depicting Stonehenge which was struck in 1796 for the Ancient Druids Universal Brethren. This was a friendly society that commissioned the medal to raise funds for the parliamentary reformer Thomas Muir, who, like Blake, had been charged with sedition, but unlike him was found guilty and sentenced to fourteen years' transportation. Blake would have sympathised with the cause and may indeed have provided a drawing for the medallist Thomas Wyon, but he would not have cared to be thought of as a Druid.

Dark, forbidding, cruel, the Stonehenge of the Romantic poets was a place of terror. It was also, noticeably, a masculine place. The qualities of the Sublime – physical power, the sense of danger, difficulty and obscurity, were male. Blake makes the distinction in *Jerusalem*:

...no more the Masculine mingle
With the feminine, but the Sublime is shut out from the
   Pathos
In howling torment.

Pathos was figuratively female for him and literally so for Wordsworth. The wandering woman is the more poignant for having the faded 'rose on her sweet cheek' set against the lurid firelight of the 'powerful circle's reddening stones', her 'sober sympathy and tranquil mind' contrast with the hectic orgy of the pagan sacrifice. The same idea occurred to Henry Thomson, whose painting, *Distress by Land*, showing a woman and her children 'defenceless before the Stonehenge storm', so closely mirrors Wordsworth that it might be taken for an illustration were it not for the fact that the Salisbury Plain poems were still unpublished in 1811. At least two Romantic novelists exploited the same dramatic contrast by bringing their heroines to Stonehenge at the climax of their stories.

The first was Fanny Burney in her last novel, *The Wanderer*, published in 1814. The book was not a success. Its length and the fact that it had been composed over a period of nearly fifteen years counted against it, but what displeased readers more was the critical view it took of English society, a view close to Wordsworth's and similarly overshadowed by recent history. Burney thought it impossible to produce 'in whatever form, any picture of actual human life, without reference to the French Revolution', which must be integral to 'every intellectual survey of the present times'. She was married to a Frenchman and had been trapped for a decade in France after 1802. She had no illusions about Napoleon. But nor was she so admiring of British life and its supposed liberties. Her heroine, the mysterious wanderer Juliet, is a refugee from the Revolution who observes fashionable society in Lewes and Brighton in all its callous frivolity. When *The Wanderer* appeared, the year before Waterloo, this was neither a patriotic nor a popular view.

The story, subtitled *Female Difficulties*, tells of Juliet's adventures in England against the background of the Terror. Towards the end, penniless and reluctantly dependent on her elderly but predatory admirer, Sir Jasper, Juliet is taken by him to Stonehenge. She walks on alone towards the 'massy ruins' and finds them 'grand and awful, though terrific rather than attractive'. As in a textbook example of the Sublime, the rough stones tower over the vulnerable figure of our heroine. But then something more interesting happens. As she sits among them Juliet begins to feel a comfort from the stones, the 'uncouth monument of ancient days' in its roughness exudes a sympathy with her own distress that calms her gradually, until 'Thought, uninterrupted and uncontrouled [*sic*], was master of her mind'. The stones retain their masculinity, but this has become a soothing and protective force. She contrasts them with Wilton, which she has just visited, and its 'appendages of luxury', which offer nothing to the suffering mind. In the two centuries since Philip Sidney had compared 'Wilton sweete' with the 'huge heapes of stones', sensibility, like the landscape, had turned inside out and could find comfort now where once there had been only chaos.

There is comfort too, of a bitter kind, in the climax of the greatest novel to invoke Stonehenge, Thomas Hardy's *Tess of the D'Urbervilles*. Although he was writing nearly a century after Fanny Burney, his novels set in the suffering and expressive landscape of Wessex belong with Blake and Wordsworth to the same Romantic tradition. Towards the end of the book Tess, who has murdered the man who seduced her, has married Angel Clare and is fleeing with him when they come, by night, to Salisbury Plain. Since Juliet was there another hundred years of landscape painting and guidebook descriptions had taken their artistic toll and overworked the image of Stonehenge into a cliché. Hardy brilliantly reawakens it by the literary equivalent of William Cunnington's technique. He brings his characters to Salisbury Plain at night so that, vast as it is, Stonehenge comes upon them suddenly. They hear the stones before they see them fully as the wind plays among them, humming like 'some gigantic one-stringed harp'. Once inside the circle, Tess lies down to sleep upon the Altar Stone. 'It is so solemn and so lonely,' she tells Angel, finding, like Juliet, some comfort in the place. As she lies there, a sacrificial victim waiting a cruel modern justice, Angel watches over her until the dawn begins to rise. 'The band of silver paleness along the east horizon made even the distant parts of the Great Plain appear dark and near; and the whole enormous landscape bore that impress of reserve, taciturnity, and hesitation which is usual just before day.' As the dawn wind falls and the sun rises, men appear from behind the megaliths. They have come to take Tess, but at Angel's request they let her sleep, standing round her in a human circle more savage and implacable than the stones. When she wakes she goes willingly with them to trial and then to be hanged. It is the climax not just of the novel but of the Romantic literary tradition that found in Stonehenge a symbol powerful enough to stand for all humanity and inhumanity and for the individual in the shadow of history.

To rise to such heights required the genius of a Wordsworth

or a Hardy. Elsewhere Stonehenge and the Druids lost a certain amount of dignity as they passed into popular Romantic culture. The English found the Sublime difficult. They much preferred the Picturesque, with its tumbledown cottages and ivied ruins. The Druids sometimes became Picturesque or, just missing the Sublime, plunged, like Gray's Bard into the gulf and became ridiculous. The Prince of Wales, later Prince Regent and then George IV, was in all things a leader of fashion. He headed the subscription list for Iolo Morganwg's *Poems Lyric and Pastoral*, followed by James Boswell, Fanny Burney, William Wilberforce and many other distinguished people who also paid for the privilege of receiving Iolo's prefatory rant against his enemies, 'the boasted laws of this land ... one REEVES [and] ... his brother *Bearmonger* of Holborn-Hill ... modern Welsh Historians, gentlemen (if they may be so called) of no conscience' and a list of many other private misfortunes and personal grudges.

By 1802 the Prince of Wales had his own bard, Edward Jones, whose book of ballads, *The Bardic Museum of Primitive British Literature*, included 'Hail, all hail to the mistletoe', a traditional Druidic song to be sung 'with dignity' and arranged for the piano. But the ultimate expression of Picturesque taste, for those who could afford it, was the landscape garden. While Humphrey Repton was creating vistas of great charm and beauty for his exclusive clientele, the more general passion for follies, artificial ruins and ornamental hermits gave rise to some curious miniature henges following the lead of the Earl of Pembroke's pioneering version at Wilton. At Alton Towers in Staffordshire the fifteenth Earl of Shrewsbury added to his collection of pagodas and fountains a 'Stonehenge' which stood between the Gothic temple and the cottage belonging to the Earl's personal harpist. It rose, not very imposingly, above the conservatory. At Swinton in Yorkshire William Danby, combining fashion with philanthropy, created work for local labourers by paying them a shilling a day to build a great oval of standing stones complete with ceremonial avenue. Like the Earl of Shrewsbury's, Danby's Stonehenge still stands and in 1993, by way of a dubious compliment to its aura of authenticity, a severed pig's head was discovered on the central altar stone.

Follies offered a rich vein of satire which nobody exploited better than Thomas Love Peacock. His novel of 1816, *Headlong Hall*, deals with the pretensions of Mr Milestone – a thinly disguised Humphrey Repton – who persuades the gullible Squire Headlong to spend a fortune on ridiculous improvements to his grounds. Peacock hits not only nails but several of the characters on the head when Mr Milestone's scheme for creating a Sublime sense of danger with a megalith, a 'ponderous stone, so exactly balanced as to be ready to fall on the head of any person who may happen to be beneath', goes wrong, with predictable results for the unfortunate house guests. Peacock's novels were part of the great late-Georgian satire boom, when caricature and cartoons flourished, yet Stonehenge itself features only rarely, for there is nothing intrinsically funny about it. It is its implacable gravity that makes it so often the foil for the comedy of contrasts and bathos. In itself it offers nothing to ridicule. Even Thomas Rowlandson, though he drew it, could not get a laugh out of it. His cartoon parson Dr Syntax, in his hopeless quest for the Picturesque, does not visit Salisbury Plain, but Rowlandson does invoke it as the background for the last plate in his darkest work, *The English Dance of Death*, where Time and Death succumb to

17. The miniature 'Stonehenge' at Alton Towers in Staffordshire, home of the Earls of Shrewsbury, was one of many late Georgian garden follies made in imitation of the original. Some were more plausible than others.

Eternity in the form of a portly angel, while in the background an assemblage of somewhat phallic megaliths collapses.

Of the various eighteenth- and nineteenth-century attempts to recreate the atmosphere of Stonehenge in three dimensions, the best and most interesting idea, though it never came to fruition, was John Britton's. The Wiltshire antiquary, topographer, historian, publisher, self-promoter and one-time showman was impressed by the models of the site made by Henry Browne. In 1822, as visitor numbers continued to rise, Browne appointed himself the first full-time guardian of Stonehenge. His models, available singly or in pairs, showed the monument as it had perhaps been originally and as it appeared in the early nineteenth century, and were based on Browne's own theories about its history. He believed it to be the last building put up before the Flood. Britton could not agree with Browne's 'very eccentric hypothesis' but thought it a pity that nobody would review the 'humble pamphlets' which he published. It was typical of Britton that his attempts to secure some recognition for Browne by 'turning his talents to use' were couched in terms that seemed to disparage him at every point, while promoting his promoter. Britton, though he was, he assured readers of the *Gentleman's Magazine* in 1825, 'urgently occupied, at least 14 hours per day with literary works and public and private engagements', tried to raise a subscription to pay Browne to produce his models. Once this was achieved through the proposed Druidical Antiquarian Company (a term, Britton explained with his usual ponderousness, that was used 'merely jocosely'), Britton himself would make them the centrepiece of a light show which would combine information and entertainment in an early form of interactive visitor centre.

18. John Britton hoped that his life-long enthusiasm for Stonehenge would be commemorated after his death with a monument in the form of a trilithon. Unfortunately funds ran short and he was buried, in 1857, in West Norwood Cemetery, under a single megalith.

Light shows were immensely popular in the Romantic period. Art and science met in these displays of (usually) backlit painting over which, by the skilful use of lamps and shutters, the moon appeared to pass behind clouds at Holyrood or distant horsemen to cross the Alps. Britton had begun his career by writing, performing and singing the commentary for one such show, the Eidophusikon. Now he came up with a plan for another such 'very interesting exhibition … of Celtic or Druidical Antiquities', to be combined with a commentary. The illuminated model of Stonehenge would no doubt have been an attraction, but the £5 subscriptions, as so often in his career, were not forthcoming. What does survive is Britton's Celtic Cabinet, an astonishing piece of furniture which he persuaded a wealthy enthusiast to commission. It incorporates a pair of Browne's models, plus another of Avebury, and it is now in the Devizes Museum in Wiltshire. The remnant of the light-show idea can be glimpsed in the glass case on top, its sides tinted different colours to suggest the various times of day. Light could be shone through them to create an atmospheric effect of dawn or sunset when the model was viewed from above. Britton, while he despaired of finding an answer to the questions it posed, never lost his enthusiasm for Stonehenge, or his passion for replicating it. In his London garden at St Pancras he created a stone circle 'intended to indicate, on a small scale, a Celtic or Druidical Temple' and at his death it was hoped to erect at least a trilithon to his memory. Yet again, however, the funds ran short and he is buried, in West Norwood cemetery in London, under a single megalith.

Among the more traditional arts, painting found Stonehenge a difficult subject. Most of the great watercolourists

19. John Britton's 'Celtic Cabinet' made in about 1824 in the shape of a trilithon. It houses a pair of Henry Browne's models of Stonehenge showing it as it was in the early nineteenth century and as he believed it to have been originally. The glass in the case on top is coloured to imitate the effects of dawn and dusk on the stones.

and many amateurs attempted it, but few distinguished themselves. Gilpin was right, it was not Picturesque, and after 1797, when the western trilithon fell, it was even less so. Many of the popular views and engravings were little more than hack work, some of them surely made not from life but from Browne's or other models, which led to even more unconvincing results. Only Samuel Palmer, the visionary artist and follower of Blake, managed to make an image of Stonehenge that was intimate, picturesque and truthful. He set it in the background of what Blake would have called 'a little moony night', a scene illustrating Milton's *Il Penseroso* and the lines:

Or let my lamp at midnight hour
Be seen in some high lonely tower

Beyond the solitary tower the outline of Stonehenge appears against the night sky seeming by comparison familiar and hence comforting. This was, Palmer explained, his intention, to evoke a scene of 'poetic loneliness – not the loneliness of the desert, but a secluded spot in a genial pastoral country, enriched also by antique relics, such as those so-called Druidic stones'.

Of those who eschewed the Picturesque and took the high road of classical history painting, the most interesting to tackle Stonehenge was another acquaintance of Blake, the best of the history painters, James Barry. He incorporated a version of it in his *King Lear Weeping over the Body of Cordelia*, painted in 1786–7 and now in Tate Britain in London. History painting, though much admired in theory, was never popular in Britain. Landscapes, portraits, narratives and animal pictures all went down better with the public and Barry died

20. James Barry's *King Lear Weeping over the Body of Cordelia*, 1786–7. Barry presents a confrontation between the old, Gothic, order and the new Classical civilization with Stonehenge an enigmatic presence in the background.

embittered and impoverished in 1806, believing himself to have been the victim of 'a dark conspiracy'. He was certainly badly treated. The Society for the Encouragement of Art in particular, as Blake noted in the margin of his copy of the *Works of Sir Joshua Reynolds*, 'Suffer'd Barry to Give them his Labour for Nothing, A Society Composed of the Flower of the English Nobility & Gentry? – Suffering an Artist to Starve'. Barry, the only artist ever to be expelled from the Royal Academy, was an example of a man with a persecution complex who was also actually persecuted. No doubt his strange appearance, 'rugged, austere and passion-beaten', not unlike a Druidical Lear, contributed to the difficulties he experienced with neighbours and critics. But he was also a man of controversial, radical views, a friend not only of Blake but of Joseph Priestley and Mary Wollstonecraft, a 'sturdy republican'. His *Lear* was painted just before the French Revolution, yet, like Wordsworth and Fanny Burney, he was thinking of the overthrow of monarchy and the rise of a new social order. Shakespeare's play, its story taken at several removes from Geoffrey of Monmouth, is scarcely a republican parable, but its end is the fall of a king, brought down by ill-judgment. In Barry's version old and new orders are painted in a way that depicts the battle of the styles, classical and Gothic, as well as the battle for the state. Lear is a primitive, wild-eyed creature, desperate and pathetic as he holds his dead daughter in his arms. His other daughters lie dead at his feet. Opposite him Edgar and Albany, who represent the new order, are painted with the 'sublime, venerable, majestic, genuine simplicity of the Grecian taste' that Barry admired.

What, in this context, Stonehenge represents is not clear. The stone circle is visible behind the human circle in the foreground. Scott Paul Gordon, who has written the fullest account of the painting as 'patriot art', is inclined to see it as a 'republican image', showing the ancient Britons resisting the invaders. That was one popular reading of the Druids and their monuments, but it seems more likely that Barry shared Blake's view and saw the monument like Lear himself as a symbol of ancient tyranny about to be overthrown. It is impossible to be sure; the scene in front of the trilithons is 'hard to decipher', as Gordon points out. This was the kind of difficulty, not knowing what was going on or what to think about it, that made the British dislike history painting.

The most popular medium of the Romantic era was water-colour and the two most successful portrayals of Stonehenge are in that medium by the two greatest British Romantic artists, J. M. W. Turner and John Constable. Turner made two views. One shows it in the distance, the other, a close-up exhibited in London at the Egyptian Halls in 1829, became the subject of an immensely popular print. It involved con-siderable artistic licence. Described fairly by the archae-ologist Christopher Chippindale as 'hopeless' in terms of accuracy, the painting deals with the problem of composi-tion by adjusting the stones, changing the shape of some and adding others, until the result is both picturesque and sublime. At Turner's Stonehenge a shepherd has been struck dead by lightning. His dog howls beside him, and around him many of his flock lie stricken, while overhead the storm rages and lightning forks across a wild sky. It is the storm, the elemental force, that makes the drama. As Ruskin later wrote, it is 'as if the whole muscular energy were writhing in every fold; and [the clouds'] fantastic and fiery volumes have a peculiar horror, an awful life'. In this extraordinary piece of painting the most transient of natural effects is prolonged indefinitely, the mental anguish of Wordsworth's wanderer is abstracted into light and air, while between the turbulent sky in the background and the scene of death and suffering in the foreground stand the all-resisting stones.

No Romantic was likely to produce a picture called 'A Fine Day at Stonehenge' and equally extreme weather characterises Constable's version, the most ambitious watercolour of his career, painted in 1835. Like his rival Turner, Constable was interested in an imagined landscape, thinking, as he told John Britton, that the 'literal representation' of Stonehenge 'as a "stone quarry" has been often enough done'. For him, too, it is the wide sky that offers the opportunity to draw on the emotions of the viewer. Once again it is stormy, but split this time not by lightning but by a double rainbow. Constable visited Stonehenge only once, in July 1820, but he did not begin planning his view of it until the end of 1832, at a time when he was much troubled physically by illness and mentally by anxiety. His work was not going well, his book *English Landscape Scenery* was a financial disaster and he feared the consequences of the great Reform Act, which would, by extending the vote, undermine, he thought, the order of society. By 1834 he felt that 'every gleam of sunshine is blighted to me … Can it … be wondered at that I paint continual storms?' If there is a political reading of his Stonehenge it is, uniquely among the Romantics, a conservative one.

The idea should not be taken too far. What Constable was painting above all was the much-discussed but seldom achieved Sublime of what he called 'the mysterious monument … unconnected with the events of past ages … [which] carries you back beyond all historical record'. Yet underlying it, surely, is the comparison with another favourite subject, both of Constable and of those who contemplated Stonehenge, Salisbury Cathedral. Since Dr Johnson had made the comparison of these two 'eminent models of art and rudeness ... the first essay, and the last perfection of architecture', it had become a tourist's cliché. Wordsworth's wanderer measures his worsening situation as he advances towards the stones and loses sight of 'the distant spire' of the cathedral, which he looks back for long after it has gone. Constable painted Salisbury Cathedral many times, culminating in the view from the water meadows of 1831, also under a stormy sky and rainbow, portraying a fragile hope in dark times as reform menaced, he thought, the established Church. In his Stonehenge the monument abides against the fleeting rainbow and the spots of time that count for human history.

Yet Stonehenge, by 1835, was on the brink of change once more, or rather the understanding of it was. Between 1831 and 1833, while Constable was working on his painting, Charles Lyell published his three-volume work, *Principles of Geology*. The time barrier that had trapped Stonehenge within biblical chronology was about to be broken as the implications of Lyell's book became more widely accepted and understood. And sensibilities were changing too. It was not until 1842 that the elderly Wordsworth finally published a version of his 'Salisbury Plain' called 'Guilt and Sorrow'. It was not a great success. His friend Dr Arnold, headmaster of Rugby College, told the disappointed poet that young people these days seldom read the classics or poetry, and 'his lads seemed to care for nothing but Bozzy's next No'. 'Can that Man's public and others of the like kind materially affect the question',

Wordsworth wondered nervously, adding, 'I am quite in the dark.' 'Bozzy' or Boz was the pseudonym of Charles Dickens. The Victorian age had arrived.

5

....

THE AGE OF DARWIN

In which *'everything is explained by geology and astronomy.'*
Benjamin Disraeli, *Tancred*

The Victorians did not lose interest in Stonehenge, in fact they visited it in ever increasing numbers, but they found it less mysterious than their predecessors had. Theirs was an age of expansion, imperial and intellectual. If there were questions still to be answered, then it was only a matter of time and science. 'Very few of the riddles which puzzled and perplexed our forefathers now remain,' the architectural historian James Fergusson remarked in the *Quarterly Review* in 1860, at the beginning of an article that went on to prove that Stonehenge was a post-Roman Buddhist temple. And as mental horizons expanded, so language grew in proportion. Among the words that were either coined or took on their modern meaning in the nineteenth century were 'archaeology', 'ethnology', 'photography', 'megalith', 'cave-man', 'dinosaur' and 'railway'. All of them had implications for Stonehenge. Poets, meanwhile, came less often to Salisbury Plain and, when they did, like Coventry Patmore's hero in *The Angel in the House*, they generally chose fine weather, unpacked a hamper beneath the shady stones and there 'in converse sweet, / Took luncheon'.

Not that this was a complacent age. Its certainties were matched by equally compelling doubts, for as science and industry transformed human experience, so they raised fundamental questions about human nature. Were we God-created beings or simply overdeveloped apes? The nature of creation itself had to be reimagined and it was geology, 'the newest and most controversial of the sciences', that first raised these important, disturbing questions. 'If only the Geologists would let me alone,' Ruskin wrote to his friend Henry Acland in 1851, '...those dreadful hammers! I hear the clink of them at the end of every cadence of the Bible verses.' That same year Matthew Arnold looked out on Dover Beach and heard 'the melancholy, long, withdrawing roar' of faith and certainty. But it was in the cliffs and fossils, these immeasurably old rocks, that profound mystery now lay. Stonehenge by comparison could be classed by Arthur Evans in the *Archaeological Review* as merely an 'antiquarian riddle'. When Darwin himself visited it in the summer of 1877 he came in search of the answer to a much smaller, if interesting question, the activity of earthworms. He drew a cross-section of one of the fallen sarsens showing how, due to the worms, it had sunk over time into the ground. The drawing appears in his last book, the improbable best-seller of 1881, *The Formation of Vegetable Mould Through the Action of Worms*.

Its diminishing mystery, however, did not prevent the Victorians from bringing the full weight of their new intellectual firepower to bear on Stonehenge. The abiding questions – How old? Who by? What for? – could be met with much more varied if not always more accurate answers. 'Time, time, time', that, as the geologist George Scrope said, was the problem. Geology had to wrestle with Archbishop

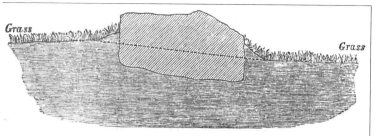

Fig. 7.

Section through one of the fallen Druidical stones at Stonehenge,
showing how much it had sunk into the ground. Scale ½ inch
to 1 foot.

21. Darwin's last book, *The Formation of Vegetable Mould through the Action of Worms*, published in 1881, included his findings from Stonehenge. It showed the stones from an unfamiliar angle, both visually and intellectually and reflected the Victorians' more pragmatic approach to the subject.

Ussher, whose 4004-year span for prehistory was becoming increasingly inadequate to cover even the known history of ancient civilisations. The most effective attempt to break the time barrier was made by Scrope's friend Charles Lyell, in his *Principles of Geology*. Like *On the Origin of Species*, more than twenty-five years later, the *Principles* was not wholly original. Much of what Lyell said had been said before. That his was the voice that made itself heard owed something to his prose style, which was persuasive and fluent, and much to his utter respectability. Despite his determination to 'free science from Moses', Lyell remained a practising Anglican all his life and he put forward his ideas in moderate, carefully referenced terms. Published by John Murray, the publisher of Walter Scott, *Principles* seemed a solid, even conservative book. It has been described as a Trojan horse and the Victorians wheeled it enthusiastically into their midst. It ran through edition after edition.

Lyell's thesis, which came to be called 'uniformitarianism', said nothing directly about creation. It worked back from the present, starting with his own field observations and going on to suggest that the same causes had had the same effects throughout time. It was volcanoes and earthquakes, sedimentation and erosion, working over immensely long periods, rather than sudden catastrophic events such as the Creation or the Flood that could best explain the strata of the earth's surface and the fossil remains within them. By now very few people believed in the Genesis story literally – the creationist Christianity which makes such a belief a tenet of faith is a relatively modern phenomenon – but Lyell replaced Genesis with a prospect of 'deep time' which had implications far beyond geology. John Herschel, the astronomer, saw that the book would 'work a complete revolution'. The young Darwin found 'it altered the whole tone of one's mind'. And many less remarkable minds were in the mood to be altered. The other secret of the *Principles'* success was timing, the historical moment that it caught, just at the dawn of the steam age. As railway lines were cut and mine shafts sunk, more people saw for themselves the rocks and the traces of ancient life within them. Industrial cities became positively competitive about their fossils, with Liverpool's tortoise footprints, found at the sandstone quarries at Storeton, countered by Manchester's much larger fossilised trees. Science had now 'descended to earth', as Michael Angelo Garvey put it in his book *The Silent Revolution*, published in 1852. Steam and electricity made it part of everyday life. 'It penetrates our mines. It enters our workshops. It speeds along with the iron courser of the rail.'

Communication was faster than ever before and the most talked-about book, a far greater sensation than *Principles of Geology* or anything by Darwin, was one that is now largely forgotten. *Vestiges of the Natural History of Creation*, which appeared anonymously in 1844, offered a general theory of everything that drew together the latest ideas in astronomy, geology, physiology, psychology, anthropology and theology. *Vestiges*, whose author was much later revealed to be Robert Chambers, a Scottish journalist with six fingers on each hand and hence a particular interest in inherited characteristics, was frankly populist in its approach. It outsold Dickens and it made evolutionary science a subject of drawing-room conversation suitable even for ladies. Prince Albert read it every afternoon to Queen Victoria and Elizabeth Barrett discussed it with Anna Jameson. *Vestiges* is the book that makes Disraeli's Lady Constance, in *Tancred*, think she knows everything:

'it is all explained. But what is most interesting, is the way in which man has been developed. You know all is development … First there was nothing, then there was something; then, I forget the next, I think there were shells, then fishes; then we came, let me see, did we come next? Never mind that; we came at last … it is all science; … Everything is proved; by geology you know.'

The implications that had lurked in Lyell's Trojan horse burst out in the *Vestiges*, along with much else. Darwin read it and found the author's geology 'bad, and his zoology far worse'. But he watched the public response closely with an eye to how his own, more carefully worked-out theories might be received. When it appeared in 1859 his *Origin of Species* generated a great wave of publicity and controversy, and it has come to be seen as the founding text of evolutionary science. 'Darwinism' was one of the new words of 1860, but the *Origin* was never a scandalous book or even a sensational one. The debate by now had its own, unstoppable momentum and it rolled through the old disciplines of theology and astronomy, as well as the new ones of anthropology and archaeology.

As for Stonehenge, which had for so long sat in the mind's eye on windswept Salisbury Plain, it was now set in a whole new intellectual landscape. Ralph Waldo Emerson, who was in Britain in 1847–8, went to visit it directly from Cambridge, where he had been much impressed by the Professor of Geology Adam Sedgwick's 'museum of megatheria and mastodons'. With this fresh in his mind, he was quite willing to believe that Stonehenge was the work of some of the 'cleverer elephants' of antiquity, but was disappointed that despite the national reverence for this 'old egg' out of which so much of its history had hatched, there was still no fully satisfactory account of it. He was baffled by 'that exhaustive British sense and perseverance, so whimsical in its choice of objects, which leaves its own Stonehenge or Choir Gaur to the rabbits, whilst it opens pyramids and uncovers Nineveh'. Indeed it is a curious fact that there was no significant excavation at Stonehenge during Queen Victoria's reign, but this was the result of circumstance rather than whimsy. In 1824 the Amesbury estate passed into the ownership of the Antrobus family, who refused almost all requests to dig. Thus while Colt Hoare and Cunnington could claim to have laid the foundations of British archaeology among the prehistoric remains of Wiltshire, the period in which archaeology came of age, when, as Emerson observed, the British were busily digging all over the world, passed this most famous and important site by almost untouched.

Yet activities elsewhere, in Nineveh and Egypt, Virginia, Devon and the Somme had far-reaching consequences for Stonehenge. Archaeology, a word redefined in 1837 by William Whewell as not merely the study of the past but specifically 'the scientific study of the remains and monuments of the prehistoric period', grew up out of the old antiquarianism and the new geology. As well as measuring and drawing monuments, the Victorians began to dig methodically, observing the strata as geologists did. It was a Dane, Christian Jürgen Thomsen, who first had the idea of keeping excavated objects together and showing them as they were found. At the royal museum in Copenhagen, where he was curator, Thomsen eschewed the narrative display style favoured by Cunnington and Colt Hoare and instead exhibited his finds as they had been uncovered. From this he developed his 'three-age' system, based on the materials used for the cutting tools found in different sites. Thus were born the Stone, Bronze and Iron Ages and for the first time there was at least an outline map for that vast and newly discovered terrain of the past before the dawn of written history. Thomsen's theories were borne out by the observations of Thomas Jefferson in the United States and Thomsen's own assistant Jens Jacob Worsaae in Denmark, establishing 'stratigraphy' as a scientific method. With Worsaae's appointment as Royal Archaeologist to Frederick VII in 1847, professional archaeology was born and in its youth the new discipline much resembled its antiquarian parent, not least in a certain flamboyance of personal style. Worsaae's appointment brought with it a splendid quasi-military uniform and on his more important excavations he liked to be accompanied by a brass band.

What the nineteenth century was discovering about the deep past, both before and after Darwin published, changed everything. 'Evolution' or 'development' became the prism through which all new discoveries were viewed and old ones re-examined. 'Primitive' peoples, the roots of language, the origins of mythology, all acquired additional interest and became informed, sometimes it might be truer to say infected, with ideas of evolutionary development. Lecturing on Stonehenge at Oxford in 1889, Arthur Evans described stone circles as if they were a living species, tracing their 'embryology' from the earlier barrows and finding some cases, such as New Grange in Ireland, of 'transitional examples' where 'the stone circle is actually seen in the act as it were of separating itself from the earth barrows'. Despite which, Evans had to admit that the mystery of Salisbury Plain remained unsolved, 'the Sphinx still sits upon those stony portals'. Indeed, as the century wore on the possible answers multiplied. Not only did time get longer but mankind's existence within it was being stretched ever further back. Since the late eighteenth century there had been finds of human bones among the remains of extinct animals in caves in France and Britain, but their implications had been either missed or vigorously denied. It became increasingly difficult to ignore them. In the Neander Valley near Düsseldorf the skull later known as Neanderthal Man was found by some limestone quarrymen in 1856. It was clear, as Boucher de Perthes, the French antiquary and archaeologist, put it, that '*Dieu est éternel, mais l'homme est bien vieux*' (God is eternal, but Man is pretty old). In 1859, the year Darwin published *Origin of Species*, this view of human antiquity was formally accepted by the Royal Society in London and by most scientists in Europe and the United States.

The most important, and level-headed, attempt to apply all the latest findings of archaeology, ethnography and anthropology to Stonehenge was made by John Lubbock, whose *Prehistoric Times as Illustrated by Ancient Remains and the Manners and Customs of Modern Savages* appeared in 1865. It revolutionised the study of prehistory, not least because he believed that 'it is wiser to confess our ignorance, than to waste valuable time in useless guesses'. Lubbock was a friend of Darwin and of Ruskin, a banker and a botanist rather than a professional archaeologist, but he had been to the Somme and excavated 'every gravel pit and section from Amiens down to the sea'. He had learned Danish in order to keep up with the developments there and as part of his research into the nature of mental processes spent three months trying – without success – to teach his poodle to read. Lubbock coined the term 'cave-man' and made the distinction within the Stone Age between the 'Palaeolithic' and 'Neolithic'.

He was a synthesiser rather than an original thinker but the weight of combined learning he brought to bear on his subject showed it in a new light. Of Stonehenge itself he came to the conclusion, based on Colt Hoare's excavations in the barrows, that it belonged to the Bronze Age. There had been only two discoveries of iron in the surrounding burial mounds and these were later interments, while fragments of bluestone and sarsen within the barrows suggested to him that they were contemporary with the monument. But it was still only a comparative chronology. Of what date they all were Lubbock could not say, only that they were probably much older than anyone had yet considered. He was prepared to countenance a past of twenty thousand years, more than three times Ussher's, but concluded shrewdly that 'it may be doubted whether even geologists yet realise the great antiquity of our race'.

As for the question of who had built Stonehenge, Lubbock took up Mr Fergusson's 'very interesting article' in the *Quarterly Review* and politely refuted it. Stonehenge could not, he argued, be post-Roman. Of the Buddhist theory, however, as of the Phoenician, he was cautiously accepting. Victorian explorers, missionaries and colonisers were travelling ever further and sending back reports that made the monuments of other civilisations increasingly well known in Britain. Stone circles were turning up all over the world. Lubbock felt that the resemblances were 'too great to be accidental'. He was, however, more cautious than another friend of Darwin, the botanist Joseph Hooker, who was in the Himalayas in 1850. Hooker had no hesitation in labelling the standing stones he saw there the 'Nurtiung Stonehenge'. This circle of granite megaliths, 'split by heat and cold water with great art' and 'erected by dint of sheer brute strength, the lever being the only aid', might suggest how Stonehenge had been built. But Lubbock was not so seduced as some by the metaphorical power of 'development', pointing out that there were differences as well as similarities between 'savage' peoples. He was not sure that they represented an earlier stage of evolution rather than merely having a different 'ethnographical characteristic'.

Lubbock was one of the great Victorian optimists, an open-minded Christian who could not believe that honest enquiry could ever damage true faith. He had none of his friend Ruskin's spiritual difficulties with hammers, but he was very worried about real hammers and their effect on Stonehenge. Tourism continued to grow and so did the popular passion for geology. The stones, by the mid-century, were beginning to suffer serious damage as more and more visitors chipped off souvenirs, and the whole site rang sometimes with the sound of banging and scraping. Meanwhile at Avebury the village, 'like some beautiful parasite', threatened to grow and overwhelm its host. 'As population increases and land grows more valuable, these ancient monuments become more and more liable to mutilation or destruction,' Lubbock noted. While the sites were still private property there was nothing to compel their owners to protect them or to prevent them from redeveloping them. Might not the government take action, he wondered, to preserve 'the graves of our ancestors' by appointing an official Conservator? They could even do as the exemplary Danes had done and purchase some of the monuments for the nation. For the moment it was only a suggestion, but one to which the energetic Lubbock would return later in the century, when he became the active as well as the intellectual hero of Victorian Stonehenge.

In the interim the emergence of professional archaeology did not result in that outbreak of intellectual clarity, harmony and pure scientific reason which might have been hoped for. While a consensus formed in favour of Lubbock's Bronze Age theory, it was by no means overwhelming. Fergusson was highly regarded and his views were influential, while catastrophists, those opposed to uniformitarianism, who believed in the creation and the Flood as single events, were still numerous. They included Henry Browne, whose theories were recounted to all visitors and upheld, after his death in 1839, by his son Joseph, who succeeded him. Most informed sources still thought that Stonehenge had been built with the help, or under the influence, of another race, with the Phoenicians still a popular choice. Charles Pearson, Professor of History at King's College, London, a firm uniformitarian, nevertheless argued for the fifth century AD and saw Stonehenge as 'a combination of the Roman circus or amphitheatre, with a development of the old sepulchral architecture, for the purposes of worship'. Outstanding among the more individual theorists was the Dean of Merton College, Oxford, Algernon Herbert, whose *Cyclops Christianus, or the supposed antiquity of Stonehenge*, appeared in 1849 and put a similar case to Charles Pearson's but in terms 'so wild and fanciful' that even Pearson felt he could not subscribe to it. Herbert thought it 'morally … impossible' that the Romans should not have mentioned Stonehenge if it was there and went on to draw elaborate conclusions from some early chronicles and the symbolism of King Arthur's Round Table.

Although stratigraphy was of no direct help in settling the questions surrounding Stonehenge while there were no digs, other new techniques, such as photography, were brought

22. *The First Preaching of Christianity in Britain*, by J. R. Herbert, 1842, from
an engraving of 1847 by Charles George Lewis. The converted Druid is
seen removing his pagan crown of oak leaves prior to receiving communion.
By the mid nineteenth century the connection between the Druids and
Stonehenge was taken for granted by everyone from Darwin to Dickens.

to bear. But like archaeology itself, these methods were no more reliable than those who deployed them and it was soon discovered that the camera can lie. Mr E. P. Loftus Brock, addressing the British Archaeological Association on his observations of 'Sunrise at Stonehenge on the Longest Day', described his attempt to assess 'with some sort of scientific accuracy' the truth or otherwise of the tradition that the sun rose directly over the Heel Stone at midsummer. With the help of Mr Howe of Newbury and his photographic apparatus, Mr Brock observed, or thought he observed, the dawn appear 'exactly over the ancient gnomen' and went home satisfied that the old story was 'verified beyond all question' not having noticed that the sun rises just to the north. In 1867 Colonel Sir Henry James, director general of another great Victorian enterprise, the Ordnance Survey, produced a full report on Stonehenge, with photographs and plans, intended as a model for his surveyors of how they might record ancient monuments. The accompanying text, however, belongs to the older tradition, comprising a lengthy series of 'notes relating to the Druids', and indeed until the 1920s prehistoric monuments were marked as 'Druidic' on Ordnance Survey maps. Flinders Petrie, the great Egyptologist, applied his 'inductive metrology' to Stonehenge and produced a more accurately measured plan than any to date. He renumbered the stones, establishing the system still in use today, and managed to demolish Stukeley's Druidical cubit, but his results remained inconclusive. He found two units of measurement, one Phoenician and the other the Roman foot. What was really needed to resolve matters, he concluded, was 'careful and intelligent digging', and this the owner refused to countenance.

Summing up the state of affairs in 1876, the antiquary

William Long – himself a supporter of the theory that Stonehenge was built by the Belgae, the inhabitants of northern Gaul – could only lament the 'dissipation of Archaeological power and … profitless "beating of the air"' which was still going on in 'the endeavour to maintain positions which the writer humbly believes to be utterly untenable'. The main position he was anxious to undermine was that of the pro-Druid school. Sir Henry James was not their only supporter and although many antiquaries had given them up – even Algernon Herbert, whatever his peculiarities, was too well versed in the classical sources to countenance them – among the general public they flourished. Every child knew that they had built Stonehenge, especially those who read Dickens's *Child's History of England.* Published in *Household Words* from 1851 to 1853, it unfolds a blood-curdling vision of prehistoric times that harps alarmingly on the 'strange and terrible religion called the Religion of the Druids', which involved horrible torture, human sacrifice and 'some kind of veneration for the Oak, and for the mistletoe'. 'These Druids built great Temples and altars, open to the sky, fragments of some of which are yet remaining,' Dickens explained. 'Stonehenge, on Salisbury Plain in Wiltshire, is the most extraordinary of these.' Bellini's opera *Norma*, which had its first performance in English at Drury Lane in 1837, casts its heroine as 'a high-priestess of the Temple of Esus', which is still usually presented as a version of Stonehenge and the Cuming Museum in south London is certainly not the only one to house a nineteenth-century collection that includes 'Druid' pottery beads. Even Darwin referred to Stonehenge in *The Formation of Vegetable Mould* as the 'Druidical stones', a phrase which must have disappointed some of his archaeological admirers, but in truth it had become generic.

Meanwhile the real Druids, or at least those who classed themselves as Druids in the nineteenth century, were flourishing, if not harmonious. The *Druid Magazine* for the year 5836 – or 1832 as it was reckoned by non-Druids – gave encouraging accounts of 'respectable parties enrolling themselves under the banner of Druidism' and of the Loyal Trafalgar Lodge at Monmouth processing to church through the town 'headed by their band'. There was a dinner afterwards. Early nineteenth-century Druid activity was still largely modelled on Freemasonry and there was an emphasis on dining, proposing toasts and awarding medals to one another. The magazine ran an article on Stonehenge which took a predictable view of its origins and followed John Wood's suggestions about its function in the 'Druidical system of education'. Between the lines, however, conflict was discernible. In 1833 there was a breakaway movement among the Wessex lodges which led to the foundation of the United Ancient Order in 1834. The *Druid Magazine* began to refer to members indulging in 'long, inconclusive and personal harangues', evoking Tacitus's descriptions of their Iron Age forebears on Mona, and by 1834 it claimed to represent the new Reformed Order of Druids. In 1836 there were bitter attacks by the editor on a rival publication launched by the Grand Lodge 'for the purpose of crushing the efforts and impugning the motives of this magazine'. Complaints of 'falsehood, vituperation and personal slander … dirty avocations [and an] … accumulation of bile and nastiness' took the edge off the concluding wish for readers to pass 'a joyous Christmas-tide, and a merry, healthful and prosperous New Year'. By 1837 the editor had been expelled from the Druids, 'by an incompetent authority', and after

1839, despite thorough constitutional revisions, the *Druid Magazine* seems to have ceased publication.

These differences were at least partly class-based, with the provincial lodges anxious to achieve financial benefits for their members which the more metropolitan Ancient Order rather despised. Another area of conflict was the question of whether they should be primarily a social and charitable society or whether they should embrace the mystical aspect of their tradition. Similar disagreements led to the foundation of the breakaway United Order of Druids (1839) and the Order of Druids (1858), which were variants on the same Masonic theme and, between schisms, dined, toasted and organised burial clubs and pension funds for one another. They all remained exclusively male, however, until 1900, when Lady Poore of Amesbury struck out for emancipation, declaring herself first Arch Druidess of the Isles at the head of her own women-only order. Yet despite all the arguing the first half of the nineteenth century was, as Ronald Hutton, author of the most recent study of the Druids ancient and modern, puts it, 'the high summer of Druidry in the English and Welsh imagination'. As the Victorian age wore on and scholarship cast an ever harsher light on their founding texts, the Druids lost some of their grip both on the national mythology and on Stonehenge. Increasingly it was as modern Romans that the imperial British liked to see themselves and those who followed such well-respected authorities as Fergusson and Petrie felt justified in taking Stonehenge with them.

But as Victoria's reign neared its end and the imperial certainties of the mid-century faded once again, Druidry acquired a different potency, one that relied even less on material facts than before. The study of evolution and anthropology cast fresh light on old customs and traditions and from the 1860s onwards there was a growing enthusiasm for artistic revivalism, of which William Morris's Arts and Crafts movement was the most famous example. In 1878 the British Folklore Society was founded. Its first president was Edward Clodd, a Darwinian agnostic and a friend of T. H. Huxley whose books included *The Childhood of Religions* and *Myths and Dreams*, studies of comparative folklore over time and across cultures. For Clodd, who described himself as an 'anthropological folklorist', these long traditions were revealing of human nature, they were there to be studied rather than believed.

That same year in New York, however, the mystic and psychic Madame Blavatsky became one of the co-founders of Theosophy, a movement which drew diametrically opposite conclusions from the same evidence and set out not merely to study ancient cultures but to seek the common truth from them until they harmonised into the 'pure colourless sunlight' of Theosophia, or the wisdom of God. Emerson became a Theosophist as did Lady Emily Lutyens. Oscar Wilde, W. B. Yeats and Bernard Shaw were all attracted by it, and it found echoes in the various Celtic revival movements at the end of the century and in the 'spook' designs of Charles Rennie Mackintosh and the Glasgow School. It had its effects, too, on Druidism. The Ancient and Archaeological Order of Druids, founded in 1874, based its rituals on early Celtic literature. The last decades of the century were cloudy with spirit photographs, ectoplasm and seances. Such eminent public figures as Sir Arthur Conan Doyle took an interest in spiritualism and the occult and the Druids could bask in a mystic aura of artistic respectability. The wilder excesses of Iolo Morganwg were forgotten and T. H. Thomas, an artist who, under the name Ardlunydd Pen-y-garn, was elected Herald Bard in 1895, had his robes redesigned by the Royal Academician Sir Hubert Herkomer and commissioned new regalia based on ancient Celtic patterns from the Welsh sculptor Sir William Goscombe John.

By now the Druids were very real indeed and although there are not authentic accounts of their presence at Stonehenge until the twentieth century, solstice celebrations became a regular event. These were hailed by Flinders Petrie and others as another traditional revival, but were, in form at least, a completely Victorian innovation. They proved popular, however, and by the time Mr Loftus Brock was making his photographic observations there was 'an enormous concourse of people, but little short of three thousand', gathered to witness them. For the rest of the year the tourists came in growing numbers. Some still brought their sketchbooks. Herschel drew Stonehenge on 12 August 1865 with the aid of a camera lucida, an optical device that throws an image on to the paper, giving a result that is somewhere between drawing and photography. His record makes a revealing point of comparison with the twentieth-century restoration, showing the trilithon – stones 21, 22 and 122 – standing in a slightly different position from the present. But for most Victorians the fashionable thing was to have one's photograph taken in front of the stones. The custodian who succeeded Joseph Browne in 1870 was a photographer, William Judd, and his photographic darkroom on wheels became a feature in its own right. The first known photograph of the monument itself is surprisingly late, a calotype, taken by W. R. Sedgfield in 1853, but had the site been less popular it might have been

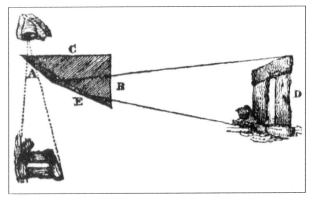

23. The astronomer John Herschel's drawing (above) was made on 12 August
1865 with a camera lucida of the sort illustrated below from the *Magazine
of Science*, 1840. The resulting image is something between a drawing and a
photograph and shows, on the left, stones 21, 22 and lintel 122 which later fell
and were restored, at a slightly different angle, in 1958.

photographed much earlier. In March 1844 William Strange-ways wrote to his nephew William Henry Fox Talbot, the pioneer of photography who lived at Lacock Abbey, not far away, asking why he didn't 'go on purpose some day & take Stonehenge'. But Talbot had already been in 1829 and found 'five carriages & thirty people, two tents pitched & a splendid cold collation' which 'wholly destroyed' the effect. He was disinclined to go again.

The lavish picnic, as rhapsodised by Coventry Patmore, became an important part of the Victorian Stonehenge visit, for the local inn, the Druid's Head, was a place of 'small accommodation' where little more than 'bread and cheese and ale' were on offer. The inn was popular at the solstice, however, when it stayed open all night attracting a somewhat raucous assembly of locals. By the end of the century celebrations had reached such a pitch that it took fifteen policemen to keep order. But it was the supposedly respectable tourists who did the real damage. Already at the time of Emerson's visit 'the marks of the mineralogist's hammer and chisel' had been visible 'on almost every stone' and the numbers continued to grow as Stonehenge felt the other side of the Victorians' changing relationship with time. While on the one hand it was being so vastly extended by geology, in everyday life it was shortening and speeding up. In 1847 the railway arrived at Salisbury and after 1857 a direct service from London made Stonehenge available to day trippers. Organised excursions ran from the station on Saturdays. 'The annihilation of space by time' was the great catchphrase of the railway builders. Space, however, was not the only thing the steam train might annihilate. Stonehenge was caught in a dangerous pincer movement between the rival London & South Western and

24. A tourist photograph of about 1896 showing the fallen western trilithon and the timber supports propping the leaning stones. The owner, Sir Edmund Antrobus, thought such measures safer and more honest than restoration.

Great Western Railway companies, which were ruthless in their attempts to penetrate one another's territory. In 1886 the LSWR proposed a line that would have ploughed straight through the Cursus. This was prevented, but ten years later the GWR put forward a plan for a line just to the east of the circle with a Stonehenge and Amesbury station. This too was avoided, but what with the railways and the litter and the local farming which, *Murray's Guide* lamented, was 'creeping over the hills, and is indeed now advanced to the very precincts of Stonehenge, within a gunshot of which are farm-buildings and cottages … whitewashed', it was clear that 'the genius of the Plain' and the other monuments were under serious threat. In the last quarter of the century a campaign began to protect them. It marked the dawn in Britain of the conservation movement and it embodied – eventually – a profound change in national attitudes to the past and to the nature of private property. John Lubbock was its leader and Stonehenge was, very often, the focus of debate.

It was Lubbock's friend Ruskin, in his *Seven Lamps of Architecture* of 1849, who first put the moral case for shared ownership of ancient buildings: 'We have no right whatever to touch them. They are not ours. They belong partly to those who built them, and partly to all the generations of mankind who are to follow us.' Twenty years later many others agreed. 'It should not be left to chance and a single person', Dickens wrote, discussing Stonehenge in *All the Year Round*, 'to do that which the State should consider it both its pride and its duty to undertake.' The immediate spur for Lubbock to act was not Stonehenge, however, but Avebury. In 1872 he received a desperate telegram from the rector warning him that part of the circle had been sold off for housing. Lubbock immediately bought all the building plots. Later he bought Silbury Hill and West Kennett Farm, which included the West Kennett Long Barrow and Hackpen Hill. He could not, however, buy everything. Instead, as Liberal MP for Maidstone, he introduced a National Monuments Preservation Bill into Parliament in 1873. It proposed a commission and a list of monuments over which it might exercise a 'power of restraint' if, after due warning, the owner intended to damage them. The bill failed. Lubbock introduced it again every year for the next six years and every time it failed. He campaigned. He read Ruskin to the House of Commons. Yet his modest proposals for the protection of ancient sites were seen as a threat to property rights and repeatedly rejected by Disraeli's Tory government.

The concept of the state having any authority at all over private property was unacceptable to many MPs and almost all of the Lords. The principle of state ownership of monuments had long been established in France, but that very fact made it unattractive to English Conservatives. There was also another more subtle point at issue. Although compulsory purchase was established to facilitate railway lines and other developments, this new law went beyond pragmatic issues and proposed to censure landowners on ethical grounds, to criticise what they did with their own property. Where would it end, Sir John Holker, the Attorney General, wondered? Such powers might be extended to 'those old abbeys and castles which were quite as interesting as the Druidical remains' even private houses, even their contents. 'If the owner of … Gainsborough's "Blue Boy" proposed to send it out of the country, were they to prevent him on the ground that the matter was one of national concern?' Sir John's fears were well grounded, for that was just where it did lead eventually. At last, in 1882, after Gladstone and the Liberals had returned to power, an Ancient Monuments Protection Act passed into law. It had no powers of compulsion but it was the thin end of that wedge the Attorney General so dreaded. Dickens, as usual, had been right about the national mood and other preservation campaigns soon followed. William Morris's Society for the Protection of Ancient Buildings had been founded in 1877 and the National Trust was established in 1895. Conservation and the idea of heritage had entered the culture.

The first Inspector of Ancient Monuments, appointed in 1888, was Lubbock's father-in-law, the archaeologist General Augustus Henry Lane Fox Pitt-Rivers, whose career, inspired directly by his reading of Darwin's *Origin of Species*, was dedicated to a theory of cultural evolution. He was another flamboyant man, whose assistants rode behind him on bicycles wearing boaters with ribbons in his heraldic colours, but he was also highly methodical. He began by approaching the owners of the twenty-nine English monuments, including Stonehenge, to be scheduled under the Act. In Sir Edmund Antrobus, however, the General met his Waterloo. Sir Edmund did not wish to place the monument in the guardianship of the commissioners, nor would he sell it to them, nor take their advice about its preservation, and he maintained this position until his death in 1898. This was the first confrontation between public and private interests at Stonehenge and it demonstrated that complex of issues that has characterised debates about conservation in general and about Stonehenge in particular ever since. Sir Edmund was a firm believer in the rights of private property but he was no philistine, unlike the public for whom the stones were supposedly being saved. A survey of Stonehenge in 1886 by the Wiltshire Archaeological and Natural History Society revealed a terrible toll of devastation. Trippers slid down the fallen western trilithon until it was worn smooth, they carved their names, they took sledgehammers to it. Sir Edmund did his best to protect the site but was told by one irate visitor that the monument was public property. No wonder he was glad it was not and the experts were not always, in his experience, much better than the outright hooligans. Among the proposals he rejected during his ownership, in addition to the many requests from archaeologists skilled and unskilled to excavate, were the replacement of the whole of the centre of the circle with concrete, the erection of a policeman's cottage next to it and the digging of a ha-ha round it, all of which would have caused irreparable damage. On the advice of his architect J. J. Cole, Antrobus adopted a solution in line with the most radical conservation thinking of the day. He did what the Society for the Preservation of Ancient Buildings would have done. He propped up some of the leaning stones with stout scaffolding that made it obvious where he had intervened. Otherwise he left it alone. 'To restoration I am distinctly opposed,' he wrote, 'but this might be considered in the light of preservation.' It could have been William Morris speaking.

After Sir Edmund's death his son, another Sir Edmund, exposed a different problem with the concept of public ownership. He offered to sell Stonehenge to the government and named a sum of £125,000, which the Chancellor of the Exchequer pronounced 'absolutely impossible'. Rumours went round the press that the stones might be sold off privately 'to some American millionaire' who would export them or that they

HOW STONEHENGE MIGHT BE POPULARISED IF THE GOVERNMENT BOUGHT IT. SUGGESTION GRATIS.

25. By the end of the nineteenth century there was increasing support for taking Stonehenge into public ownership. When this did happen, some decades later, the result was, as *Punch* anticipated, mixed.

might be used as advertising hoardings. So, as the century drew to a close, nothing was resolved. Stonehenge was still largely unprotected in law and in practice from the crowds, who were now joined by soldiers from the military camps at Bulford. In 1897 the War Office opened negotiations with local landowners and by 1902 it had 43,000 acres of Salisbury Plain to the north of Stonehenge which were used for infantry manoeuvres. A branch line brought more trippers on the railway to Amesbury. Then came the motor car. Easter 1899 saw the Automobile Association hold a rally at Stonehenge. By now the solstice was a cacophony of 'bicycle bells ... coach horns [and] ... the brutal staccato notes of a banjo' issuing from a crowd made up of locals, soldiers, tourists, 'snapshotters' and possibly Druids. An earlier, less scientific age would have read an ominous significance into the events of the dark and stormy night of 31 December 1900. On this last day of the nineteenth century, in a howling gale, an upright in the outer sarsen circle, number 22 in Petrie's scheme, fell. It took its lintel with it, which broke in two. These were the first stones to fall since 1797 and they left the monument sadly depleted. Three weeks later, at Osborne on the Isle of Wight, the old Queen died. For many of her subjects, who had known no other monarch, it was as if 'some monstrous reversal in the course of nature' had occurred. Hubert Herkomer, designer of the Herald Bard's robes, was one of two artists summoned to paint her on her deathbed. Her reign had seen Stonehenge better and more fully understood than before. It had set it in a broader intellectual and scientific context, in geological rather than biblical time, measured it more accurately, photographed it and compared it with similar monuments all over the world. Despite which, the departing Victorians left

Stonehenge more damaged and more vulnerable than any previous age.

'So does Time ruthlessly destroy his romances,' wrote Thomas Hardy. Hardy, a Victorian as well as a Romantic, was profoundly affected by the consequences of Darwinism. His writing is saturated with the influence of evolutionary theory and he was haunted by the terrible price his generation paid for their increased knowledge. Like Huxley, he saw that 'the "fittest" which survives in the struggle for existence may be, and often is, the ethically worst', while the best and purest, like Tess, last of the dying line of the D'Urbervilles, may be driven to extinction. The species that had, in its infancy, built Stonehenge was now, he believed, 'too extremely developed for its corporeal conditions … this planet does not supply the materials for happiness'. In taking Tess to her fate at the Altar Stone, Hardy set out merely, as he thought, 'what everybody nowadays thinks and feels', the cruelty of the human condition. It was not only a romantic tradition that died with Tess but a certain intellectual innocence.

6

ARCHAEOLOGY, ASTRONOMY AND
THE AGE OF AQUARIUS

'At Stonehenge no antiquarian cause is ever finally lost.'
John Michell, *Megalithomania*

As a new century dawned it was obvious that something had
to be done about Stonehenge. What Sir Edmund Antrobus
did was to put up a fence and impose an admission charge. For
the first time in history free access to the stones was stopped.
No matter that it was done to protect them, or that, as Lady
Antrobus wrote in the guide book, the barrier was 'composed
of lightest barbed wire of a neutral tint, and absolutely invis-
ible at a distance', it caused uproar. The Commons Preservation Society, John Lubbock (now Lord Avebury), Flinders
Petrie, the National Trust and Amesbury Parish Council
were among those who saw it as an unwarrantable act of
enclosure. In fact Stonehenge had never been on common
land and, despite a writ being issued against Sir Edmund
by Flinders Petrie and others in 1904, no legal case could be
brought. The dispute, however, set the tone for the century.
Who was to own Stonehenge, who was to visit it, when and
on what terms, were questions that remained unsettled into
the next millennium. In all its long history this twentieth

26. George MacGregor Reid and his fellow members of the Universal Bond of the Sons of Men celebrating the summer solstice, in 1913 or 1914 in front of curious onlookers. In both years 'riotous scenes' later occurred and the celebrants were ejected from the site.

century of the Christian era was the best of times and the worst of times. Great advances in understanding and appreciation were countered by irreversible damage and a struggle for ownership that occasionally became violent. Some of the scenes that have taken place on Salisbury Plain in living memory are like Blakean visions of apocalypse. Razor wire and searchlights have surrounded the stones, and police helicopters have throbbed overhead, drowning out the Druid rituals, while fighting broke out nearby.

For better and worse, this was the century that brought professional archaeology to Stonehenge. Between 1901 and 1994 there were 123 digs and other 'interventions', some of them now seen to have been highly destructive. The first excavations, however, which took place in 1901, were among the least invasive and the best. Once the beleaguered Sir Edmund had fought off the unwanted advice of Flinders Petrie and others he did what his late father would have done. He turned for help to William Morris's Society for the Preservation of Ancient Buildings and to the Arts and Crafts architect Detmar Blow. For the first time in two centuries architectural expertise was applied to Stonehenge and Blow urged the need for 'experienced craftsmen' to work on the site. He undertook operations with William Gowland. Gowland was an antiquary and a professor at the School of Mines who had spent sixteen years in Japan investigating burial mounds and laying the intellectual foundations for Japanese archaeology. Neither there nor in England has he yet received the credit he deserves. Gowland and Blow shored up some of the stones with timber, deciding to move only stone 56 of the Great Trilithon, which was tilting rapidly and bearing down on a bluestone. While restoring it to its upright position, Gowland dug a small area around its base and, working on the principles he had established in Japan, sifted what he found, recorded its location to within a few inches and published his findings in months. It was a standard that sadly few of the professionals who followed him were to match, but it made a resounding case for archaeology.

From this little dig a vast amount was discovered and questions that had puzzled generations of antiquaries were answered almost overnight. In the stone hole Blow and Gowland found the tools the workmen had used, the stone mauls or hammerstones that had shaped the sarsen and the antler picks with which the chalk had been dug. The stone hole, Gowland noticed, had been cut with a slope down one side to create a ramp in order to slide the upright into place. This explained how the stones had first been raised. Blow's assistant, Basil Stallybrass, worked out by experiment how the tooling had been done with quartzite hammerstones. He compared their effect with other possible tools until he matched the result exactly. From the fact that the nearest blue-stone, 68, was set in the rubble infill for stone 56, Gowland deduced that the bluestones had been placed in their present position after the sarsens, thus answering one of the most teasing questions of the previous century. He found no metal tools or artefacts and so concluded that Stonehenge was Neolithic, a work of native Britons, dating from about 1800 BC. It was a brisk, modestly presented piece of work that marked a gigantic leap in knowledge and understanding.

It was not enough, however, to allay suspicion about Sir Edmund's worthiness as a custodian. Attempts continued to bring Stonehenge under public control and in 1913 it was scheduled, compulsorily, under the Ancient Monuments Act, thus preventing the owner from demolishing or exporting it, which he had never intended to do. Sir Edmund, meanwhile, who shared the family dislike of officialdom, joined the Ancient Order of Druids, into which Winston Churchill was initiated a few years later. The Ancient Order came to celebrate at Stonehenge in 1905 and for some years afterwards, affording their detractors an easy target by wearing false beards but otherwise causing no trouble. The same could not be said of George MacGregor Reid and his Universal Bond of the Sons of Men. Reid was a believer in natural medicine and universal religion rumoured to have invented the tonic wine Sanatogen. It was with him that modern Druidry began its move away from the fraternal Masonic model back to the radical, countercultural style of Iolo Morganwg. Reid believed that the Druids were the British interpreters of the one original faith and that Stonehenge was its prime site. The Universal Bond accordingly set off from their headquarters at Clapham in their distinctive Indian-style costumes and held their ceremonies at the solstice from 1909 onwards. In 1912, however, there was a dispute with Sir Edmund about whether they should pay the admission fee and the next year the police were called. The same undignified scene was repeated with even greater acrimony the following year, with Reid haranguing the curious onlookers and pronouncing terrible curses on the Antrobus family.

Overall, however, the most intrusive presence at Edwardian Stonehenge was the military. Infantry manoeuvres made the ground shake. Army buildings sprouted up at Larkhill, to the north, and were accompanied after 1910 by a new phenomenon, the aeroplane hangar. Planes flew over the stones, occasionally crashing nearby, and manoeuvres increased as events in Europe moved inexorably towards war. By 1914 the old order in England was already under sentence and it required no Druidic curse to bring it down. Sir Edmund's son was killed at Ypres in 1915. He himself died seven months later and the Amesbury estate, like so many others, was broken up. Stonehenge, with the parcel of land immediately surrounding it, was put up for auction at Salisbury and bought, on impulse, by a local man, Cecil Chubb, for £6,600. As the war went on the army camps sprawled. An aerodrome was built and tanks rolled within yards of Stonehenge, where it now sat, fenced off on its shrivelled site, like some shorn Samson in captivity. Then at last, in October 1918, just before the Armistice, came the moment that Charles Dickens, John Lubbock, Flinders Petrie and many others had longed for. Chubb decided to make a gift of Stonehenge to the nation. The title deeds were handed over to the Commissioner of Works in an elaborate ceremony and the stones were at last public property. But the public is a hydra-headed entity. Its ownership of Stonehenge brought a change of difficulties rather than a solution, difficulties which began, inevitably perhaps, with the Druids. In the summer of 1926 a series of misunderstandings with the Office of Works led to a confrontation in which George MacGregor Reid incited a crowd of onlookers to storm the fence. It was the first but by no means the last violent invasion of Stonehenge. The removal of the remaining right of way across the site caused more dispute with local people. For the archaeologists, however, national ownership was a boon, removing all obstacles to the large-scale excavation they had been itching to do for so long. Digging began in November 1919.

William Gowland was too old to undertake the work

and it was his assistant, William Hawley, who took charge, with a brief to 'excavate Stonehenge completely and at the minimum expense'. The verdicts of later archaeologists on what followed vary from unfortunate to catastrophic. Many now feel that Hawley was left to flounder by the Society of Antiquaries, to whom he was supposed to report, and that his efforts, unlike those of some of his successors, were competent and responsible. Others, including Christopher Chippindale, refer to this as the period which saw 'the destruction of half Stonehenge'. Operations started with some of the more precariously leaning stones and their lintels, which were put straight and set in concrete. Then the digging began. Hawley and his assistant, R. S. Newall, worked for seven years with diminishing enthusiasm. One problem was the lack of spectacular discoveries, the glamorous treasure that might capture the imagination of the public which now owned Stonehenge. In November 1922 Howard Carter opened the tomb of Tutankhamun and the world was dazzled by the face of the boy king. Hawley and Newall, meanwhile, carried on turning up broken flints, Roman coins, fragments of pottery and old clay pipes. Even the Society of Antiquaries lost interest.

Hawley nevertheless made important discoveries. Encouraged by Newall, he decided to look for the ring of holes that John Aubrey had mentioned and found them. They had been filled in but were detectable when the ground was struck with steel rods. There were fifty-six, of which Hawley and Newall excavated thirty-two, finding them to be filled with chalk and cremated remains. As well as the Aubrey Holes, as they decided to call them, they found the Y and Z holes. Discoveries in what Hawley named the 'Stonehenge layer', the debris that lies just beneath the turf, enabled him to establish that the outer earthwork was older than the stone circle, for there were chips of stone in the filling. It was the beginning of another immensely important realisation, that Stonehenge was not all of one date, that it had been built in phases over time. Hawley suggested three phases (three being the number beloved of archaeology) and it is a schema which, much modified, still obtains today. He also kept detailed notes while he carried on stoically with his increasingly thankless task. Newall, meanwhile, seems to have been the first to propose the now popular theory that the ritual significance of Stonehenge was based on alignment with the midwinter rather than the midsummer sun.

Yet undoubtedly he and Hawley did a lot of damage as they stripped, sieved and sorted. Digging, as Stukeley had noted, is like dissection, it destroys its own evidence. The finds that were later reburied as being of 'no interest' might in their original positions have interested the age of carbon-dating very much. It was a pity, too, that when Hawley sent the two skeletons he discovered to the Royal College of Surgeons he did not pack them up better, for they were broken in the post. All in all, it was fortunate that the Society of Antiquaries let the operation fizzle out in 1926. More light was cast on Stonehenge in these years from less obvious directions. In 1923 the geologist Herbert Thomas proved, to almost everybody's satisfaction, that the bluestones had come from the Preseli Hills. Two years later Group Captain Gilbert Insall, one of the most decorated pilots of the First World War took a single-seater Sopwith Snipe over the stones and noticed, about a mile and a half away from them, evidence on the ground that something similar in scale and shape had once stood there. Insall's observation was the beginning of the

27. Once Stonehenge became public property restoration work began. This photograph was taken in 1919, when several leaning stones were straightened and set in concrete. It shows a lintel being adjusted.

discovery of what became known as Woodhenge, a bank and ditch within which were concentric circles of pits that had once held wooden posts. The structure dates from about 2300 BC and buried at its centre is the skeleton of a child with its skull split in two, an apparently macabre relic, which has since turned out to be capable of less sinister interpretations. The story of the excavation of the Woodhenge site is a subject in itself. As far as Stonehenge was concerned, the effect of this and Insall's later aerial find, the wooden circle at Arminghall in Norfolk, was to place it in a wider landscape of prehistoric architecture. Once again the language had to expand and in 1932 Thomas Kendrick of the British Museum coined the word 'henge' as a generic term for this kind of construction, which is found almost exclusively in Britain. The new word was helpful up to a point, but his definition of a henge as a circular enclosure with a ditch inside a bank does not in fact apply to Stonehenge, where the bank is inside the ditch. So although there would be no such concept without it, Stonehenge itself is not, as far as archaeologists are concerned, a true henge. But archaeologists, even once they got their hands on them, did not have a monopoly on the stones.

The Druids of course persevered. *The Druid*, the magazine of the Ancient Order, was founded in 1907. It carried advertisements of interest to readers in search of a 'Druidic Haircut and shave', a Druid convalescent home or a bona fide sample of magic cork. The editors promised, or warned, that simply because it was now known that 'the erection of the Sacred Circles was not the work of Druid hands' the brethren would not lose interest in Stonehenge; 'On the contrary…' More generally, there was a febrile romanticism abroad in Britain between the wars. It ran through modern art and literature and had its effects on science. Even at the heart of archaeology, wisps of the mystical continued to find their way through scientific rationalism, like smoke through a loosely piled bonfire. At Glastonbury, where the abbey was placed in the care of a charitable trust in 1908 with a view to its better preservation, excavations were undertaken by Frederick Bligh Bond, who delighted the trustees by discovering, almost at once, the sites of the long-lost Edgar and Loretto Chapels. They were less delighted when, in 1918, Bond published *The Gate of Remembrance*, an account of how he had located the chapels through a series of seances in which he had contacted one of the monks who had constructed the abbey and who also revealed the sacred geometry of its layout. Despite the intervention of Conan Doyle, the Bishop of Wells was not placated and Bond was eventually sacked. But a mystical view of the ancient past was gaining ground. For those who read Jung and believed (as Bligh Bond did) in a mental world of archetypes and the collective unconscious, there was a place in the modern world where science and mysticism might meet and intertwine. In the early 1920s Alfred Watkins was busy near Salisbury and elsewhere developing the theory of ley lines and in 1936 the Reverend C. C. Dobson revisited the old Glastonbury foundation myths in *Did Our Lord Visit Britain as they say in Cornwall and Somerset?*, which quickly ran into six editions.

Artists, too, returned to Stonehenge. If they found it less forbidding than the Romantics had, they were perhaps more moved by it, for it seemed to speak a visual language they could understand. In 1921 the young Henry Moore visited the stones by night. The sight of them in moonlight made a profound and lasting impression. It helped to form his sense of the possibilities of sculpture in landscape, of how art set within nature could become monumental. Like Barbara Hepworth, he saw a connection by descent between himself and the creators of the stone circles, between the mute mystery of Stonehenge and the abstractions of twentieth-century art. So, too, did the painter Paul Nash. In his *Equivalents for the Megaliths* of 1935, one of a series of pictures inspired by a visit to Avebury, he set an enigmatic group of objects against the Wiltshire downs.

At Stonehenge itself, however, under the care of the Office of Works, circumstances were becoming ever less conducive to artistic contemplation; in fact they were, as the architect Clough Williams-Ellis put it in 1928, 'intolerable'. 'The Stonehenge Café, the derelict hangars of an aerodrome; a collection of huts … spiked iron railings and a turnstile … a picture-postcard kiosk; and a brand new bungalow' were among the eyesores captured in a single snapshot from the road. There was widespread criticism and the prime minister, Stanley Baldwin, announced, 'The solitude of Stonehenge should be restored … to ensure that our posterity will see it against the sky in lonely majesty.' An appeal was launched in 1927 to enable the National Trust to buy nearly 1,500 acres of land around the stones, which it duly did. In 1931 the last of the Ancient Monuments Acts was passed, prompted largely by the problems besetting Stonehenge and Avebury. The law, however, had few teeth and visitors were becoming more numerous and more intrusive. Increasingly they came by car. In H. G. Wells's novel of 1922, *Secret Places of the Heart*, in which the plot centres on a visit to Stonehenge, one of the characters watches a little boy who is less than impressed with his visit and prefers to inspect the parked cars. 'Old stones are just old stones to him. But motor cars are gods.' Indeed, the stones appeared not just in modern art but on artistic advertising posters, like McKnight Kauffer's, for Shell petrol. Road traffic now became, as it remains, the chief obstacle to creating – or restoring – a suitable setting for Stonehenge, while those motorists who were interested in old stones did not expect to sacrifice the car in order to see them. In 1935 the first car park was built.

Four years later, with the Second World War, came another blow to the ancient landscape as giant rotivators rolled across Salisbury Plain, ploughing up whatever lay beneath ground level, making the downland over to crops for much-needed food. By the time peace returned in 1945 the setting of Stonehenge fell still further short of Stanley Baldwin's vision. Clough Williams-Ellis surveyed the 'tankdromes, dumps and hutments', the debris of conflict which 'we are assured are "merely temporary"' but which often turned out to be permanent, not to mention the accompanying 'hordes of heedless and destructive and very gallant young men who would bomb or trample [national treasures] into nothing as gaily as you or I would smash plates in a … fun fair'. And if the army was sometimes careless, the Ministry of Works (as it became in 1940), with its official archaeological view, was in some ways not much better. In 1949 the artist John Piper found his visit to Stonehenge depressing. He described it in the *Architectural Review*, where his article followed pictures of a terrifyingly antiseptic school at Stevenage, the first of the post-war new towns. Piper lamented 'this guilty age of orders and self accusations', in which imagination was still on the ration and the official guide to Stonehenge was largely devoted to the negative task of dispelling romance and popular myths, especially,

How we treat "Places of Historic Interest and Natural Beauty."

DERELICT AERODROME

HUTS

"STONEHENGE CAFÉ"

THE CIRCLE

NOTICE ANNOUNCING "Site for A.A Telephone box"

LEVELLED SPACE (presumed hard Tennis Court)

NEW BUNGALOW

Stonehenge.

[The label Café has been applied in error to the wrong building. It belongs to that on the extreme right.]

28. The presentation of the site was considered unsatisfactory as early as 1928 when the architect Clough Williams-Ellis published this critique in his book *England and the Octopus.*

29. Edward McKnight Kauffer's poster for Shell was printed in 1931. Soon all too many people were taking advantage of the invitation to visit by car and traffic management has been a problem ever since.

of course, the Druids. 'We are permitted to call Stonehenge beautiful or ugly at will,' he wrote, 'but are warned that it is not the point about it; we refer to its atmosphere of worship at our own risk, on the same terms as we leave our car in the car-park … the archaeologists have had a great deal to put up with at Stonehenge', he added drily, 'and this is their reply'. Archaeology marched on undeterred, but its steady rise in the post-war period was accompanied by a growing murmur of dissent from its orthodoxies and resentment of its occasional arrogance.

Digging began again in 1950, supervised by three professional archaeologists, an 'informal committee' appointed by the Society of Antiquaries; Richard Atkinson, Stuart Piggott and J. F. S. Stone, a local man who had recently excavated the Cursus. It was to be Atkinson who dominated not just the work at Stonehenge but the post-war image of archaeology. Often on television wielding his cigarette holder as he dug into Silbury Hill or got a team of public schoolboys to demonstrate how the bluestones had been moved, he was suave and authoritative. The first of the post-war investigations was into two of the Aubrey Holes that Hawley had left intact. They revealed the same sort of mixture of infill and human remains as the others but there was now a new way of understanding such previously puzzling material. Just the year before, at the University of Chicago, the chemist Willard Libby had invented a method of dating material by its carbon content. Although this was still an imprecise technique which has since been much refined, it was a huge advance for archaeology. Libby returned a date of 1848+/-275 BC for the Stonehenge samples. Atkinson and Piggott, conscious of the damage done by their predecessors, restricted themselves to the smallest possible areas for their excavations. Their principal achievement was to develop, modify and add detail to Hawley's three-phase outline. They also discovered the Q and R holes, which once held an earlier bluestone setting, and Stone, in his work at the Cursus, found bluestone fragments, suggesting that perhaps there had been a bluestone structure there that was later dismantled and moved.

One of Atkinson's greatest discoveries, however, was not the result of excavation. It was made in the same way that Aubrey had found Avebury, simply by looking at the familiar with fresh eyes. He was photographing the inscription on stone 53, which may be the sixteenth-century artist Lucas de Heere's graffito, and he chose a moment late on a summer afternoon, when the raking sun would show it most clearly. Through his viewfinder Atkinson saw a short dagger carved on the stone. Nearby were the outlines of four Bronze Age axes. Once noticed, the carvings started to appear elsewhere. A visiting schoolboy found one on stone 4. The axes were of an Irish type. The dagger, however, was of a kind not found in northern Europe but related to examples from Greece and Mycenae. Atkinson assumed that it was carved 'within the lifetime of someone who was personally familiar with this type of weapon in its homeland', which was a large assumption given that objects may travel and survive far beyond the ken of their first users. If he was right, however, this meant the carving was no later than 1470 BC. Whatever they meant, the carvings were, at last, a discovery with some visual appeal and they caught the public imagination, which was further fired in 1956 by Atkinson's book *Stonehenge*. It instantly became the standard work. Not only was Atkinson popular for his appearances in the still-novel medium of television, he wrote well and with none of the drabness that pervaded the official guidebook. 'Of the stones themselves,' he commented in his introduction, 'no words of mine can properly describe the subtle varieties of texture and colour, or the uncountable effects of shifting light and shade … silvery grey … in sunlight, which lightens to an almost metallic bluish-white against a background of storm clouds.'

The book is chiefly devoted to a factual account of his own and others' work, but passion and imagination keep breaking through. In describing stone 36, a bluestone that had once served as a lintel, Atkinson could not help but see it through the eyes of a generation that had grown up with the abstract sculpture of Henry Moore. He found evidence in it of 'feeling for form and design'. He was ungenerous, however, towards his predecessor Hawley, describing his excavations as 'one of the more melancholy chapters in the long history of the monument', without acknowledging what he had taken from them himself. Hawley's fault, according to Atkinson, was his fear of speculation or 'any kind of working hypothesis'. Atkinson, however, erred somewhat in the opposite direction, allowing the axes to light a Stukeleyesque chain of association in his mind. He concluded:

> *I believe that Stonehenge itself is evidence for the concentration of political power … in the hands of a single man, who alone could create and maintain the conditions necessary for this great undertaking. Who he was … we shall never know … Yet who but he should sleep, like Arthur or Barbarossa, in the quiet darkness of a sarsen vault beneath the mountainous pile of Silbury Hill? And is not Stonehenge itself his memorial?*

There was little more to support Atkinson's theory of Mycenaean influence than the Reverend C. C. Dobson's, which at least had a tradition behind it. Yet he was by now the acknowledged expert. He had, or it was assumed he had, a full set of detailed notes which would be written up and published in due course as the definitive study.

While they transformed the public understanding of the monument the archaeologists were also overseeing its physical transformation into the Stonehenge we see today. Restoration work began in 1958, when the stones that had fallen in 1797 and 1900, for which there was historical evidence of their original positions, were re-erected. HEAVE-HO AT STONE-HENGE the local paper trumpeted, over photographs of the Ministry of Works' 70-ton crane winching them up. This, along with the straightening and resetting of three more leaning stones in 1959 was as far as it was considered proper to take the reconstruction. Unfortunately, during the 'heave-ho' phase stone 22 struck the upright stone 23 a glancing blow and in March 1963 that in turn fell over. Its re-erection and concreting were the last of the physical adjustments to the stones to date and it was decided that further work should be limited to 'what is required to ensure the safety and good display of the monument'. Thus it was returned, physically, to more or less the same state as it appears in depictions from Lucas de Heere's time. Intellectually and perhaps less fortunately, it had been returned to the age of Inigo Jones, when it was thought impossible that such a work could be the product of a native pre-classical civilisation. Informed opinion was for Atkinson's Mycenaeans. 'We must look to the literate civilisations of the Mediterranean,' wrote Stone, or, as Atkinson put it, '*Ex oriente lux*'.

Archaeology had now largely succeeded, as far as the general public was concerned, in wresting Stonehenge from the Druids and it felt secure in victory. 'Intellectually', as Christopher Chippindale put it, there was no dispute. The stones 'belonged to the archaeologists, as the experts in these matters', and the Ministry of Works took its cue from them. From their point of view, they had been magnanimous in allowing the Druids to continue to hold celebrations. Over the years these had gone off largely without incident, albeit also without MacGregor Reid and the Universal Bond, who had been refused permission to distribute their *Druid's Journal* in 1932, prompting another outbreak of cursing and their permanent withdrawal from Stonehenge. Meanwhile the Ancient Order of Druid Hermetists, founded in the later 1930s, partly inspired by Reid, carried on celebrating throughout the Second World War. More schisms, Reid's death in 1946 and the withdrawal of the 'fraternal' or Masonic-style orders from Stonehenge meant that from 1956 onwards the only order left at the solstice was the Circle of the Universal Bond, founded by Reid's son, Robert. Robert, a former diplomat, was adroit at avoiding conflict with the authorities.

By 1961, however, in the view of Glyn Daniel, editor of the archaeological journal *Antiquity*, the solstice was getting out of hand. 'We are no spoilsport', he announced in the editorial plural, but the Druids were 'foolish people confusing fact with fiction' and they should, he recommended, be kept out. With hindsight Daniel can be seen to have overplayed his hand. In fact it was not the Druids but the spectators who were the issue. Crowds at the solstice had been getting bigger since the early 1950s. The age of folk and jazz festivals was dawning and large open-air events were popular with the young, and not only for fun. The first Aldermaston March, run by the newly formed Campaign for Nuclear Disarmament, took place in 1958. As post-war austerity eased and the end of rationing finally came into view, there was a bohemianism about, an atmosphere of anti-establishment protest, political and artistic. Thousands of people were coming to the solstice and there had indeed been a certain amount of trouble, much harped on by the newspapers. It was due partly to students and largely to drunken soldiers from the army base, who harassed the morris dancers and laughed at the Druids. It was not their fault but, as the Chief Constable of Wiltshire put it, 'so long as there were Druids about, there would be a substantial body of weirdies making a thundering nuisance of themselves'. In 1962, partly as a result of Daniel's lobbying, a temporary electrified fence was installed to keep the public out, although, to Daniel's annoyance, a group of Druids was allowed in. The arrangement failed and by midsummer 1966 much stronger measures were in force. As the *Salisbury Journal* reported, 'Military police were everywhere … dog-handlers patrolled the … wire perimeter … the whole of the monument and its concentration-camp barbed-wire entanglements were floodlit throughout the night.' It would be difficult to know what more the authorities could have done to turn the stones into an icon of anti-establishment protest. And so, in the 1960s, began the battle, cultural and sometimes physical, for the soul of Stonehenge.

From a practical point of view, however, it was not the solstice-goers who were the problem. It was the daily tramp of the paying public that was wearing the ground away to mud. In 1963 the turf and topsoil inside the circle were removed and replaced with clinker from the Melksham gasworks which was overlaid with orange gravel. To add to this eyesore, in 1968 new visitor facilities, a larger car park and more lavatories were built and a tunnel was dug under the A344, where the ever-growing volume of traffic had made it dangerous for tourists to cross. The arrangement, always rather drab, has not worn well and now has all the allure of a motorway underpass. Described by a Parliamentary Committee in 1993 as a 'national disgrace', it is still in situ. Yet as so often in the twentieth century's faltering relationship with Stonehenge, ineptitude on one front was accompanied by profound insight on another. During the excavations for the car park the archaeologist Faith Vatcher found the post holes that are now the most ancient known features of the site, proving that the area near Stonehenge had been inhabited since the early Mesolithic age.

By the mid-sixties, however, the assault on archaeology's intellectual dominance had begun. It did not in the event come from Druids, jazz fans or disaffected students, but from science. The decade saw the dawning not only of the Age of Aquarius, but also of the space age and at Stonehenge the two met. In 1966 the English astronomer Gerald Hawkins, a professor at Boston University, published *Stonehenge Decoded*, which caused a sensation and knocked Professor Atkinson's *Stonehenge* smartly from its position as the most popular work on the subject. Reading Hawkins's book today, what is most striking is its tone of prelapsarian awe at the might of his computer. The IBM 704, Hawkins told his readers, most of whom had never seen a computer, consisted of about twenty units the size of filing cabinets, used roughly seventy horsepower of electricity, operated at 'a speed approaching that of light' and 'does not make mistakes'. Hawkins first plotted 165 recognised positions on the Stonehenge site, 'stones, stone holes, other holes, mounds', and got 'the machine', as he rather dramatically referred to it, to work out their astronomical alignments, if any. The results were remarkable. 'Not one of the most significant Stonehenge positions failed to line up with another to point to some unique sun or moon position.' Hawkins's conclusion, after many more plottings and readings, was that 'Stonehenge was an observatory … deliberately, accurately, skilfully oriented', and that the Aubrey Holes were designed to predict lunar eclipses on a fifty-six year cycle, a cycle only recently known to modern astronomers.

The book appeared at the height of the space race, three years before the first moon landings, and it made Stonehenge at once topical and modern. It also made it romantic again in both old and new ways. It connected it – by implication at least – with the Unidentified Flying Objects recently observed over Salisbury Plain, especially the Warminster Thing, a combination of lights and sounds that appeared between Stonehenge and Glastonbury and had – allegedly – been captured on film the year before. At the same time Hawkins's observatory theory restored the older vision of an ancient native civilisation, a race of wise astronomer-priests, which had haunted the stones, on and off, since Stukeley's day. Astronomical explanations of Stonehenge, though fiercely resisted by archaeologists, were not of course new. Stukeley himself first noticed the general correspondence with the midsummer sunrise, which John Smith had worked out more precisely. The eighteenth-century itinerant scientist John Waltire had called Stonehenge 'a vast Theodolite for observing the motions of the heavens' and Duke's *Druidical Temples of Wiltshire* cast the monuments of the plain as components in a giant orrery.

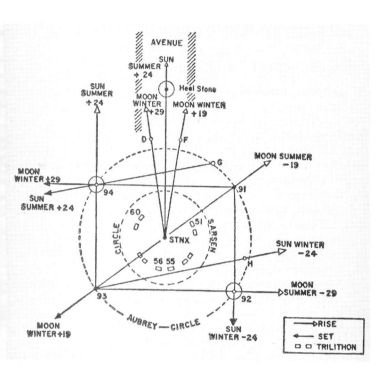

30. A diagram from the astronomer Gerald Hawkins's *Stonehenge Decoded* of 1966, showing the alignments he had found by computer analysis. An instant best-seller the book launched a heated debate between archaeologists and astronomers that continues today.

It was in 1906 that the first professional astronomer turned his attention to Stonehenge. Sir Norman Lockyer, founding editor of *Nature* magazine, published *Stonehenge and Other British Stone Monuments Astronomically Considered*, in which he found the stones to be aligned on an annual cycle running from May to November to May. Archaeologists in general and Atkinson in particular had been contemptuously dismissive of Lockyer. But other powerful voices were now raised in his defence. Academic astronomers were reassessing his work overall, finding it sound in principle if insecure in detail, and reprinting his books. By 1966 if Hawkins was the loudest proponent of the astronomical theory he was by no means alone. That same year C. A. 'Peter' Newham published an article in Lockyer's old magazine, *Nature*, called 'Stonehenge a Neolithic observatory', in which he suggested that the post holes near the entrance were used for observing moonrises over several 18.6-year cycles and pointed out that the long sides of the Station Stone rectangle had a lunar alignment. Then in 1967 Alexander Thom, formerly Professor of Engineering at Oxford University, published *Megalithic Sites in Britain*. He had spent more than a decade measuring stone circles and other monuments and come to believe that, as Clive Ruggles later put it, '"megalithic man" laid out configurations of standing stones all over Britain using precisely defined units of measurement and particular geometrical constructions, and carried out meticulous observations of the sun, moon and stars'.

This sudden onslaught on the archaeological certainties of the last half-century caused uproar. Hawkins, Newham and Thom were not writing in any spirit of hostility towards archaeology, but the archaeologists took their work in a remarkably personal and defensive way, with little attempt to address the argument. As the Marxist archaeologist Gordon Childe, who had read some of Thom's early findings, put it, 'many [archaeologists] when faced with mathematical symbols which they do not understand have aroused in them severe emotions … and it is only fair to say that this is the attitude that archaeologists are likely to display at the start'. The row was indeed highly emotional. It lasted for decades and did nothing for archaeology's claims to scientific objectivity. It also cast little light on the facts. To form a considered view of the astronomical arguments requires an understanding of both archaeology and astronomy, as well as a good grasp of physics and more than a passing familiarity with statistics and probability theory. Nobody who leapt into the fray in the 1960s and 1970s had all of these qualifications and some of them had none. Readers possessed of such advantages are referred to the bibliography. But the facts were not quite the point. At issue were two things. One was the status of archaeology itself, so recently established as a science and now under attack from another, much older and purer scientific discipline. The other was the past. For archaeologists, the world that had produced Stonehenge was populated by simple, culturally primitive people, 'mere barbarians' as Atkinson was reduced to calling them in one of his responses. A view of culture as progress, as social Darwinism and all that that implied about human nature and civilisation, was being questioned.

In an effort to achieve a resolution of the conflict that was raging through the pages of his journal *Antiquity*, Glyn Daniel commissioned another eminent astronomer, Sir Fred Hoyle, to go over the evidence. Having done so, Hoyle decided, embarrassingly, that Hawkins was, basically, right. Daniel was forced to publish Hoyle's conclusion that 'It is implausible to argue that a people ignorant of astronomy chose positions for the stones that happened by chance to display great astronomical subtlety.' If it were merely a question of superimposing his own knowledge on prehistoric evidence, as had been alleged, then why, he asked, was he unable to obtain similar results elsewhere, at Avebury, for example? Astronomical alignments were more reliable, Hoyle concluded, than the deductions of archaeologists, for they spoke for themselves: 'The wonder of it is that the message is still there, almost as clear as it was in the beginning.' So it was that by the end of the 1960s a significant breach had been opened in the academic orthodoxy. Through this opening all those who disliked the Ministry of Works and its ethos, the artists, mystics, countercultural philosophers, rock musicians, pyramidologists, flying saucer watchers, 'acid-fuelled readers of the *International Times*', sceptics and of course the Druids, could regain entry to the cultural property of Stonehenge. They flooded in.

No single person did more to marshal the forces of the anti-establishment intelligentsia than John Michell. Born in 1933 in London, Michell was educated at Eton and Cambridge before serving in the Royal Navy and then in the Civil Service as a Russian interpreter during the Cold War. Described as 'a radical traditionalist', he is thoroughly au fait with the establishment he mistrusts. In elegant prose that never lost its temper or its sense of humour, he addressed his readers on 'the many aspects of human experience and discovery not covered by conventional modern science, particularly in relation to ancient philosophy'. In 1969, the year that saw another storming of Stonehenge at the solstice, he published *The View over Atlantis*, which became, as Ronald Hutton said, 'the founding document of the earth mysteries movement'. In it he introduced a new generation to the work of Aubrey and Stukeley and revived the reputation of Alfred Watkins. Watkins's theory of ley lines was based on the belief that 'the early inhabitants of Britain deliberately placed mounds, camps and standing stones across the landscape in straight lines'. These lines, down which psychic energy flowed, could still be traced in the siting of Christian churches, the keeps of medieval castles and on a line from Stonehenge to Old Sarum to Salisbury Cathedral. It was a belief that had attracted renewed interest since the 1950s, especially among those who had observed the Warminster manifestations, which were on the Stonehenge–Glastonbury ley. *The View over Atlantis*, however, popularised the theory. It rescued Bligh Bond from obscurity and promoted the writings of Alexander Thom. The book was a compendium of occult knowledge, occult in the sense that it had been deliberately hidden or ignored by conventional science. It ranged from Stukeley's Druidism to the psychoanalyst Wilhelm Reich's theory of the orgone in a quest for clues to the ancient tradition by which, Michell believed, the monuments of prehistory had been raised 'with the help of some remarkable power'. Modern humanity, in Michell's vision, lived in 'a vast ruin', the remnant of 'A great scientific instrument [which] lies sprawled over the entire surface of the globe'. Of Stonehenge itself, he wrote that it was possessed of 'its own hidden geometry, a pattern of energy that spirals away from the centre to spread over the surrounding countryside', and is reflected in the design of Glastonbury Abbey.

If only a few were prepared to go so far, there were many who found Michell's resistance to academic overspecialisation, the dividing of knowledge into 'ever more isolated categories', attractive. His underlying thesis is that civilisation moves in what he characterises as Platonic cycles rather than Hobbesian straight lines, and thus beliefs may pass with time from lunacy to heresy to orthodoxy. It has been proved in part by his own work. The sombre note on which he ended *The View over Atlantis* may have been hippie nonsense in 1969, but it seems prophetic now:

> *the earth is slowly dying of poison, a process whose continuation is inevitably associated with many of the fundamental assumptions of the modern technological civilization. The radical alterations to the social structure necessary to avert the approaching crisis may lie beyond reach of achievement.*

In 1977 Michell published *Secrets of the Stones: The Story of Astro-Archaeology*, in which he surveyed the intellectual battle for Stonehenge and other megalithic sites. By then astro-archaeology, a word probably first used in print in 1971, was well advanced on the journey from heresy to orthodoxy. Indeed at this point there was a lively traffic in both directions, for academic archaeology was somewhat in disarray. Improved methods of carbon-dating, developed in the late 1960s, had pushed the chronology of Stonehenge back in time, making Atkinson's Mycenaean theory untenable. This left what another distinguished archaeologist, Colin Renfrew, described as 'a void in European prehistoric studies'. If knowledge had not been diffused from the Mediterranean to the primitive people of Wessex, how had Stonehenge happened?

Euan MacKie, head of Archaeology and Anthropology at the Hunterian Museum, caused panic in some quarters by suggesting that maybe the builders had indeed been native astronomer priests and therefore the Iron Age Druids really were their descendants after all. Richard Atkinson, having excavated Silbury Hill and failed to find his sleeping king, underwent a Damascene conversion to Thom's theory of the megalithic yard, helped him to carry out a survey of Stonehenge and made a public retraction of his earlier views in the *Journal of Astronomy*.

But if archaeology was at something of a crossroads at Stonehenge, it was not at a standstill. In 1978 Atkinson and J. G. Evans reopened a trench of 1954 and found a skeleton buried some time between 2400 and 2140 BC. It was the young man killed by arrows now known as the Stonehenge Archer. The following year saw another of those coincidences of insight and idiocy that characterised the century. An official of the General Post Office drew a line on a map for a new telephone cable which happened to run across Stonehenge. Not until the GPO's bright yellow digger was within yards of the Heel Stone, and then entirely by chance, was it spotted and stopped. Mike Pitts, an archaeologist from the Avebury Museum, mounted a 'rescue dig' on the site and found evidence that there had once been a pair to the Heel Stone. This was a substantial discovery. It removed one of the principal objections to the idea of the solstice orientation, the fact that the sun does not rise directly over the Heel Stone. This, it now seemed, might be deliberate. The sun was meant to be seen rising between a pair of stones. If indeed, a later archaeological report conceded, the purpose of Stonehenge had been to celebrate the midsummer sunrise, then 'the positioning of the two stones here would have achieved that aim'. It was a substantial point to astro-archaeology.

In 1974 the countercultural appeal of the solstice crystallised into the first Stonehenge Free Festival. An outdoor music event based a few hundred yards to the west of the stones, it was soon a major fixture in the alternative summer season. It was relatively small and good-humoured. In the sweltering summer of 1976 the fire brigade played water on the crowd as they danced and the police used their headlights to illuminate the stage. Over the next decade the event got bigger, benefiting from the nearby Glastonbury Festival, which had been held at the solstice since 1971. Some of the stars came over to play to the free festival crowd and Stonehenge underwent another of its periodic transformations, becoming now an icon of rock culture. Black Sabbath's 1983 album *Born Again* included a track called 'Stonehenge' and when they took the album on tour they decided to base their set on the stones. The tour turned out to be memorable, but not in the way the band had hoped. According to the singer Ian Gillan, it was the bassist, Geezer Butler – who had presumably never been to Stonehenge – who told the designers he wanted it 'life size'. Butler blamed an error in the conversion to metric. Whoever's fault it was, the band ended up on the road with a set that filled three containers and was too big for any stage. They used as much of it as they could, edging awkwardly between megaliths as they performed. But the group who welded Stonehenge forever to the heavy metal scene was Spinal Tap, stars of Rob Reiner's eponymous film of 1984 about 'one of England's loudest bands', a mock documentary that became a classic and eerily prefigured the Sabbath's experience. In a sequence first shot before the *Born Again* tour, Spinal Tap find that owing to a mix-up between feet and inches the Great Trilithon, which descends on to the stage at the climax of their act, is only 18 inches high. Attempts to contextualise it with a leprechaun dance make matters worse but perhaps the real genius of the scene is the Stonehenge lyric – a masterpiece of haute rock bathos:

Stonehenge, where the demons dwell
Where the banshees live and they do live well
Stonehenge
Where a man is a man and the children dance to
    the pipes of Pan … etc.

Not everyone saw the funny side. On 1 April 1984 management of the Stonehenge site passed into the hands of a new quango, English Heritage. By now the national mood had darkened. The first half of the 1980s saw inner city riots in London and Liverpool. At Greenham Common in Berkshire, where US cruise missiles were based, a long residential protest began in 1981, organised by women who linked hands to 'embrace the base'. There were violent conflicts involving the miners at Orgreave in 1984 and the print workers at Wapping in 1986. Laws against squatting were tightened and numbers of young people took to the road in travellers' convoys. The 1984 Stonehenge Festival was the biggest ever, with as many as a hundred thousand people coming and going. It was peaceful and the sun shone. But it was to be the last time the public were allowed access to the stones for the solstice until the next millennium. By 1985 the travellers' convoys were attracting a great deal of opposition. Moving round the country through the summer from festival to festival, they were accused of creating noise and mess, intimidating local people, sponging off social security, damaging land and generally being a nuisance. The chairman of English Heritage, Lord Montagu of Beaulieu, came under pressure from local Wiltshire landowners to suppress the festival and he agreed. Injunctions were taken out against eighty-three named individuals. Police in full riot gear with helicopter support set out to stop the festival-goers' convoy as it headed for Stonehenge. They met it at Cholderton on the Wiltshire border and, after a prolonged stand-off, fighting broke out. The Battle of the Beanfield, as it became known, was little reported. The police had warned journalists to stay away for their own safety. There were four hundred and twenty arrests on charges of obstruction and unlawful assembly. Glyn Daniel noted with satisfaction in *Antiquity* that the Wiltshire police had 'dealt firmly with the invaders'. However, when those charged appeared in the local magistrates' court the Earl of Cardigan, secretary of the Marlborough Conservative Association, who had witnessed the events, took a different view. He thought the police had been brutal and the whole scene 'grotesque'. His fellow landowners were furious, but the Earl made it known that 'If I see a policeman truncheoning a woman I feel I'm entitled to say it is not a good thing.' Charges were dropped. Some of the convoy limped off to Lord Cardigan's land, where he refused the police access to evict them.

If 1985 was, as John Michell wrote, 'the saddest year in the history of the monument' to date, those that followed were worse. In 1986 the Public Order Act was passed, its provisions intended, among other things, to give the authorities more control over events like the solstice. Stonehenge 'freedom marches' set off from all over the country. The act

31. The violent confrontation of June 1985 between police and travellers attempting to get to Stonehenge was little reported. Tim Malyon, who took this picture, was one of the few photographers present. He later agreed with Lord Cardigan that at the Battle of the Beanfield, as it became known, the police had used undue force.

was controversial in many ways but one of its most peculiar unintended consequences was a Druid revival arguably bigger than anything since Iolo Morganwg's day. Throughout the century the new Druid orders had moved ever further from the Victorian model of friendly societies with an essentially Christian culture towards a broader spirituality and interest in the occult. The rituals of Robert Reid's Universal Bond dwelt less on God and increasingly on the elements, human potential and 'generalised cosmic forces'. Its influences included the ritual magician Aleister Crowley and among its supporters was Gerald Gardner, promulgator of Wicca, or modern witchcraft, the only religion ever to be founded in England.

Paganism and earth mysteries infused the new Druidry, but without making it more harmonious than the old. Robert Reid had not been on speaking terms with his father, George, and in 1964 Robert's own death occasioned another schism when the Order of Ovates, Bards and Druids split from the Universal Bond and went off to hold their solstice celebrations at Glastonbury. In 1988 Philip Carr-Gomm refounded the Order of Ovates, Bards and Druids, which had lapsed in 1975, and it rapidly became the largest of the Druid orders devoted to spiritual matters, while in the mid-1990s women members left to found the Cotswold Order of Druids and the British Druid Order. These were all in the broadest sense counter cultural, opposing or at least offering a critique of the prevailing social order. But after 1986 three new orders were formed that concerned themselves particularly with reclaiming the right to use Stonehenge as a national temple: GOD (the Glastonbury Order of Druids), SOD (the Secular Order of Druids) and LAW (the Loyal Arthurian Warband). 'Stonehenge … belongs to the world,' wrote Tim Sebastian, founder of SOD, 'we who live in this sacred Isle are its custodians and we should be its users, not for trivia, not for political ideology, and not for profit, but for the encouragement of the youth of the world … STONEHENGE BELONGS TO THE FUTURE.'

For several years after the Beanfield there was an uneasy and intermittent peace at the solstice, with more trouble breaking out in 1988. English Heritage offered a limited number of tickets, which were accepted by local people, archaeologists and some Druids, while others stuck to the principle of open access. Attempts to control the event became increasingly heavy-handed. By 1988 Amesbury residents were complaining that they had to carry identity cards and that there were roadblocks round the town. Then in 1989 English Heritage clamped down, introducing an annual four-mile exclusion zone secured by razor wire, patrolled by helicopters and enforced with multiple arrests. When authority becomes such a cumbersome Goliath it is easily thrown off balance and it encountered its David in John Rothwell, former soldier, biker and founder of LAW, a revival of Geoffrey of Monmouth's Arthurian vision of Stonehenge. Rothwell changed his name legally to Arthur Pendragon and acquired the sword from John Boorman's film *Excalibur*. Dressed in flowing robes and living for months at the site, surviving on handouts, King Arthur's message to visitors was 'Don't pay, walk away.' Each year he and the Warband attempted to breach the exclusion zone and were regularly arrested under the Public Order Act, which states that any group of more than two people moving in the same direction may be counted as a procession and arrested as a threat to public order. One year King Arthur said it was a picnic, not a procession, and so was arrested for possession of an offensive weapon (Excalibur) instead. In

1995 he performed a citizen's arrest on the policeman who was trying to arrest him, under 'Articles 9, 10, 11 and 14 of the European Convention of Human Rights'. It was a campaign of peaceful – and witty – civil resistance that owed as much to Gandhi as to Camelot and it made the authorities look increasingly ridiculous.

As another decade turned, things seemed grim on many fronts, but not all. Archaeology and archaeologists were changing. There had never been total support for Daniel's dogmatic line. The ageing and increasingly mellow Richard Atkinson had always rather liked the idea of the festival, while the rising generation were more sympathetic to their contemporaries. A young archaeologist, Michael Heaton, wrote to the *Guardian* in 1985 that 'The damage, if any, done to Stonehenge [by the festival] is piffling in comparison to the damage done by the Ministry of Defence, but because it is done by "hippies" … it is singled out for … hysteria.' In 1990 Christopher Chippindale edited *Who Owns Stonehenge?*, a collection of essays that brought archaeologists, Druids and others together on paper at least. Two years after that a minibus full of young archaeologists entered into the Arthurian spirit by turning up at the exclusion-zone perimeter and announcing their intention of going in singly at fifty-yard intervals (thereby not constituting a procession). They were told they would be arrested anyway. More generally among those who had grown up in the age of ley lines and sacred geometry, even if they did not believe in them, there was a willingness to see Stonehenge – and all ancient monuments – in a broader context as part of a connected landscape that had been resonant to its creators with metaphysical meaning. Another of those cycles of intellectual fashion that interest John Michell was turning, bringing archaeology back to Stukeley's point of view, only now it was called phenomenology.

Then, in 1992, a new chief executive officer of English Heritage was appointed, Jocelyn Stevens. Stevens decided to tackle Stonehenge. Physically the site was still a mess. The orange gravel had been taken up in 1978 and turf relaid, but at the same time a permanent fence was erected to prevent the public from going in among the stones. Meanwhile the roads were ever more intrusive, the visitor centre was run down and the solstice an annual embarrassment. Intellectually things were not much better. Not everybody had been as scrupulous as Gowland about keeping notes. Atkinson and Piggott had not collated their findings with the earlier work and Atkinson's long-promised publication had yet to appear. The archaeological records were scattered and no attempt had been made to coordinate the findings made since the site became public property. Stevens initiated the assembly of a full archive and of the collaborative project that became *Stonehenge in Its Landscape: Twentieth-century Excavations*, by Rosamund Cleal and others. Its appearance in 1995 was another great advance in the understanding of Stonehenge and it incorporated all that was known to date, but it was more than a synthesis of past research. It included the latest attempt to establish an exact chronology. This was done using carbon-dating techniques and probability theory combined in OxCal, a software program developed at the Oxford Radiocarbon Accelerator Unit. The results were dramatic. They set Stonehenge back in time another thousand years. The implications were as if, Mike Pitts wrote, 'we picked up Europe's most daring Gothic cathedral and dropped it into the Dark Ages'. The other great discovery that Cleal and her co-authors made was as startling in its way, if dismaying. Richard Atkinson, who had never made any of his research material available to the project, died just as the book was being completed. When his executors handed over his papers, it was found that although they included notebooks containing 'hundreds of measurements', it was also the case that, as *Stonehenge in Its Landscape* records with chilling understatement, 'as far as could be ascertained there are no details of what they are, or from where or how they had been calculated'. In other words, the information for which archaeology had waited for nearly half a century was, when it came, useless. *Stonehenge in Its Landscape*, however, was a triumph of scholarship and gave fresh impetus to Stonehenge studies. No more digging was done, but archaeology had been learning throughout the century to make increasing use of less invasive methods, such as photography, field walking, geophysical surveying and caesium gradiometers. There were also 'finds' to be made far from Salisbury Plain. One of the skeletons Hawley had sent to the Royal College of Surgeons, which was thought to have been destroyed by bombing in the Second World War, turned up unscathed in the Natural History Museum, where it was rediscovered by Mike Pitts and given a radiocarbon date of about AD 150.

But as more questions were being answered about its past, the future of Stonehenge continued unresolved. Jocelyn Stevens found that the physical state of the monument was much more difficult to improve. In 1984 the Stonehenge Study Group had been set up to consider possible options and in 1986 Stonehenge became a UNESCO World Heritage Site. By 1991 it was attracting 615,000 visitors a year, but still they could do no more than park in the ugly car park, look at the stones across the fence and tramp round the dreary visitor centre. The problem was the roads. The A344 runs just yards from the stones down to a dangerous junction with the A303, the main route to the south-west of England, which is always busy and in summer often jammed. It was generally agreed that for the sake of Stonehenge the roads needed to be moved, closed or buried in tunnels to minimise their impact. For the sake of local people and the national transport system, the A303 needed to be doubled in size, while for everyone's sake the visitor centre ought to be improved.

Throughout the 1990s proposals were put forward for a new centre at various places to the north and the east. The site moved so often that Lord St John of Fawsley, who had been Minister for the Arts, suggested to the House of Lords that the best design would be a wigwam. There were proposals for the diversion of the A303 or its burial in a tunnel. Conferences were held, surveys commissioned and many petitions were signed. But the interests of archaeology, tourism, local residents and the Department of Transport proved impossible to reconcile. In 1997, with the election of a Labour government, the House of Lords took the opportunity to go over the whole question and appeal to the new administration to resolve the situation. Wayland Kennet, chairman of the Amesbury Society, spoke in favour of a long, bored tunnel for the A303 and a visitor centre at Countess to the east. Others felt that the tunnel, however long, with its necessary ventilation shafts and large entrance ways, would be intrusive, while for many the cost was prohibitive. In April 1999 the government rose to the Lords' challenge and the Stonehenge Master Plan was launched by English Heritage as 'a means of rescuing the stones and the 451 scheduled monuments that surround them'.

An attempt to involve all the interested parties, including the National Trust, the local council, the Highways Agency and others, it was born of an age when attitudes to the public sector were changing again, with increasing emphasis on public–private partnerships and business models for management. Accordingly, the first proposal of the Master Plan was to design a logo – to be registered as a trademark. The next stage was to be 'an international marketing campaign to find a commercial operator to design, develop and run a new visitor centre'. In the event no such operator emerged. UNESCO was critical but powerless and, as the century neared its end, confusion and acrimony reigned. At last, in December 1999, a final draft of the Stonehenge Plan was presented to Chris Smith, then Secretary of State at the Department of the Environment. It recognised that the World Heritage Site had to be treated as a whole, rather than merely focusing on the monument itself, and as such it received a wide welcome. Less welcome, in many quarters, was the proposal to solve the A303 problem by doubling the size of the road and burying it in twin 'cut and cover' tunnels past the monument.

On the question of the solstice, the last decade of the century also saw progress, eventually. The campaign for free access had been unremitting and the annual protests had become associated with other campaigns, notably those against road building, which saw young – and some not so young – protesters willing to live in trees or holes in the ground to try and prevent, physically, the building of the Newbury Bypass in Berkshire and the M3 at Twyford Down in Hampshire, where the new motorway was set to destroy part of a designated Site of Special Scientific Interest. King Arthur and LAW were active at Newbury, getting themselves arrested as often as possible in order to overload the justice system. By now Stonehenge had become an internationally recognised symbol of protest inspiring the artist and anti-nuclear campaigner Adam Horowitz to start work on his *Stonefridge* in Santa Fe, New Mexico. A circle of old refrigerators, surrounding an inner group of refrigerator trilithons, it is aligned on the Los Alamos National Laboratories. Back in Britain in 1994, in another attempt to deal with mass protests, the Criminal Justice Act was passed, creating an offence of 'trespassory assembly', which allowed the police to arrest groups of twenty or more if 'serious disruption to the life of the community' was likely to ensue.

On the tenth anniversary of the Battle of the Beanfield, 1 June 1995, there was a Free Stonehenge demonstration at the monument. The police cautioned the crowd, most of whom dispersed, except for two, Margaret Jones and Richard Lloyd, who decided to 'put their rights to the test' and were duly arrested. Arthur and his Warband promptly went to London and chained up the front door of English Heritage's headquarters. Then, while the machinery of the law ground on, there was a gradual easing in relations. Arthur proposed a meeting – at a round table, naturally – to bring English Heritage, the National Trust, police, local people, councillors and assorted Druids together. Those who made the first tentative overtures from both sides felt obliged to be secretive. The English Heritage archaeologists feared for their jobs and the various protest groups for their credibility. Finally an official meeting was held in 1996, with 'numerous heated exchanges, plus the occasional walk-out for dramatic effect', but two years later things had improved sufficiently for the authorities to allow some access on the same ticket basis as before. This caused more rifts among the Druids, some of whom felt that limited access was better than none, while others stuck to the principle of free entry for all.

Finally, in 1999, the case of the Stonehenge Two reached the House of Lords. The Lords overturned the conviction, upheld the protesters' right to demonstrate and criticised the Criminal Justice Act, pointing out that it would in theory mean that 'two friends who meet in the street and stop to talk are committing a trespass … and so too a group of members of the Salvation Army singing hymns'. As the Lord Chancellor, Derry Irvine, put it in his verdict, this was 'an issue of fundamental constitutional importance … the public highway is a public place which the public may enjoy for any reasonable purpose'. That year the perimeter fence was broken again but it was the last violent solstice. From 2000 onwards, English Heritage would be obliged to arrange open access. That public, for whose ownership of Stonehenge the early twentieth century had campaigned, would finally regain the right of free entry to the stones themselves for one day a year.

Elsewhere the wheels of intellectual orthodoxy kept on turning, until the astronomical heresy arrived inside the gates of the establishment. A consensus was gradually emerging among archaeologists that even if not all the precise alignments insisted on by Hoyle and Hawkins could be justified, there was more than a merely general or accidental coincidence between megalithic monuments and astronomical positions. In particular Thom's theory that foresights, markers some distance from individual monuments, were used to establish alignments was widely accepted. In 1990 the Royal Mail issued a set of stamps to celebrate the history of astronomy which featured Stonehenge on the 37p design under the phases of the moon and in 1999 Clive Ruggles of Leicester University was appointed the world's first professor of astro-archaeology. The transformation of Edwardian lunacy into twenty-first-century science was complete, if not universally popular. 'Stonehenge,' Ruggles noted, 'continues

31. The astronomical interpretation became ever more widely accepted and in 1990 Stonehenge was included in a set of Royal Mail stamps celebrating astronomy.

to be the very icon of archaeo-astronomy ... while astronomy continues to be the very bane of many archaeologists' existence.' It was, however, amid relative peace and harmony that preparations got under way for the new century and to mark it a Welsh group, Menter Preseli, successfully applied for a £100,000 Lottery Millennium Festival grant to take a bluestone from the Preseli Hills to Salisbury Plain, 'using only information available at the time Stonehenge was built'.

7

....

THE NEW MILLENNIUM

'An embarrassing, abominable, inexcusable mess…'
Mike Pitts, Editor, British Archaeology

This chapter might begin exactly the same as the last, for as another new century dawned it was once again evident that something, or rather something else, had to be done about Stonehenge. Public ownership, if it had not failed, had not succeeded as its supporters had hoped, and if the Druids and the solstice-goers had been placated for the moment, nobody else had. In January 2000 a letter to *The Times* from the British Archaeological Trust, the Campaign for the Preservation of Rural England, Friends of the Earth, Save Our Sacred Sites and others appealed to UNESCO to put Stonehenge on its list of 'monuments at risk'. They argued that not only was the present situation untenable, but the proposed construction of shallow cut and cover tunnels across the World Heritage Site, and the scarring, noise, light and other pollution that would result from them, would cause irreparable damage. English Heritage replied a few days later that a longer tunnel, bored at a deeper level, was too expensive and would create problems of its own. An element of compromise, they felt, was essential but there was no meeting of minds, only an increasingly ill-tempered stalemate.

Meanwhile the Menter Preseli group were working on their millennium project to transport a stone from Wales to Wiltshire by Stone Age means. This turned out to be more difficult than expected. Even after Health and Safety inspectors had banned authentic Neolithic costumes and insisted on gloves, the volunteers found the eight-foot megalith almost impossible to move and the press coverage went from enthusiastic to satirical. 'Rock won't roll', *The Times* chortled. By June the team had got as far as the sea, but having managed to get the stone going the next problem, inevitably, was stopping it. As it was being floated across the Bristol Channel on a raft between two 'Stone Age' boats, it slipped and sank to the bottom. A muffled titter went round the country. Undaunted, the team recovered their megalith and the project struggled on into the summer, by which time the use of divers, cranes, tug boats and nylon netting had thoroughly undermined any claim to authenticity. Eventually it was the insurers who called a halt. Two things, however, had been proved, one obvious and one less so. The first was that people in the Stone Age were much more adept at moving stones than they were over four thousand years later, and the second was that the idea of operating 'using only information available at the time Stonehenge was built' was intellectually as well as practically flawed. It is impossible to know with certainty what was known in the past, only that certain things were not known.

The first, perhaps the only, good news for Stonehenge in 2000 came with the summer solstice, for which English Heritage now felt obliged to provide 'managed open access'. If it did so with lightly gritted teeth, the event was nevertheless a great success, going off without trouble, as it has done ever since. It attracted a crowd of about six thousand that year, rising to about thirty thousand by 2007. Visitors for the rest of the year, however, still faced a disappointing experience. The average time spent at Stonehenge is now a mere twenty minutes and for most tour operators it is no more than a 'toilet stop' between London and Bath. Tourism received a further blow early in 2001, when Brian Edwards of the University of the West of England gave his view to the newspapers that the alterations to Stonehenge had been so extensive that it was now an entirely modern monument 'created by the heritage industry' and merely foisted on unsuspecting tourists as prehistoric. English Heritage promised a new guidebook, which duly appeared in 2005, and does make reference to the twentieth-century restorations.

All this time the much-criticised Stonehenge Plan was still in place. Its solution to the visitor centre problem was to situate it at Countess, just outside the eastern edge of the World Heritage Site. By July, however, it was apparent that the great hoped-for commercial opportunity to manage it as a complex of shops and restaurants had failed to materialise and so English Heritage took matters into its own hands and bought the land. The following April, 2001, brought the announcement that Denton Corker Marshall, a firm of Australian architects, had won the contract to design the new centre. Their proposal for a building in a nest of concentric curves, set into the landscape with only a series of slender white ribs visible through the covering turf, looked elegant and imaginative, but it could not by itself provide a solution. Well might ICOMOS – the International Council on Monuments and Sites, which advises UNESCO – appeal to the British government for 'joined-up thinking'. It urged consideration

33. The government announcement in December 2007 that it would not fund
the latest proposals for a road tunnel under Stonehenge made the rest of the
English Heritage management plan for a new visitor centre unworkable.
This provoked various reactions. Louis Hellman's Martians, who appeared in
the *Architects' Journal*, summed up one of the most common.

to be given equally to the three possible solutions to the road problem available since the 1990s: the 2-kilometre cut and cover tunnel, a 2-kilometre bored tunnel and a 4-kilometre bored tunnel. The cut and cover option was the most damaging to the archaeology of the site and the 4-kilometre tunnel the most expensive. In December 2002 the Department of Transport announced plans for 2.1-kilometre bored tunnel. This was supported by English Heritage but questioned or opposed by many other groups and individuals.

Prominent among them was the newly formed Stonehenge Alliance, founded by Wayland Kennet. The Alliance argued that the necessary excavations would be the largest man-made interventions ever on Salisbury Plain. They would include permanently floodlit tunnel entrances too close to the stones and their effects would be irreversible. The National Trust, which had been acquiring more land around the central site from time to time since its initial purchase and now owned nearly 2,000 acres, began to voice reservations. The Council for British Archaeology went so far as to lodge a formal complaint. In February 2004 a public inquiry into the A303 proposals opened in Salisbury and in August English Heritage applied for planning permission for its visitor centre. The next summer the government announced the outcome of the public inquiry, which was that, despite evidence given by conservationists and others, the short bored tunnel was the best option. It added, however, that since costs had risen during the time the matter had been debated, there was to be a review of all the possible options to assess whether the tunnel represented value for money. That same month Salisbury District Council turned down English Heritage's plans for the visitor centre. Another of those expensive diminishing circles of argument that have characterised the modern mismanagement of Stonehenge was complete.

In January 2006 the Highways Agency announced a public consultation on five options. It was to be a process that demonstrated the truth of Winston Churchill's remark that 'Democracy is the worst form of government, except for all those other forms that have been tried from time to time.' Some consideration was given to all proposed solutions, beyond the five to be assessed in detail, whether they came from public bodies or private individuals, leaving, as the report's authors put it with, perhaps, a wan attempt at humour, 'no stone unturned'. Even the suggestion that a combined solution to the road versus heritage problem might be to turn Stonehenge itself into a giant traffic roundabout was put on the record. The opinions of local people, archaeologists, the army, the National Trust, the Society of Antiquaries and many others more or less expert were taken into account. In the century since Sir Edmund Antrobus put up the first fence, the number and nature of the interested parties had changed and multiplied beyond recognition. Not only was the archaeology of Stonehenge better understood, it was understood as part of a wider prehistoric landscape that should be preserved and reconnected. Meanwhile the ecological concerns that had been the province of specialists and hippies in the 1960s were now universally respected. All this was to the good, but it made decisions difficult. The Royal Society for the Protection of Birds, Britain's largest charity, mobilised its members in defence of the skylarks, corn buntings, lapwings and barn owls which would be disturbed by any diversion of the existing road to the north or the south. Beyond the World Heritage Site itself there was now also, to the north, the Salisbury Plain Area of Conservation, the Special Protection Area and a Site of Special Scientific Interest, 'the largest known expanse of unimproved chalk downland in Europe', which was home to, among others, the rare Desmoulin whorl snail and many water voles. The report also included a section headed 'Effects on Bats'. Pitted against this complex and delicate world of natural and archaeological rarities was the unquestioned need to improve the traffic flow on the A303.

Overall the consultation revealed a discrepancy between the views of local people, who were mostly concerned with relieving traffic congestion and faintly resentful of the interference of an 'elite' of outsiders, and the other respondents. Among the latter there were some surprising bedfellows, with the Royal Automobile Club and the Alliance of Pagan and Druid Communities finding themselves in close agreement. In the end there was a 58 per cent majority in favour of the existing scheme, the shorter 2.1-kilometre bored tunnel. Among the dissenters, however, who found the consultation process limited and flawed, were some formidable opponents. They included the National Trust, without whose agreement it was hard to see how any plan could proceed, for the Trust holds its land inalienably, the Royal Archaeological Institute, the Stonehenge Alliance, Friends of the Earth and ICOMOS. In June 2006, just in time for the solstice and shortly before the consultation findings were announced, the National Trust issued a press release that was also a rallying cry. It explained that it had for more than seventy years 'been acquiring parts of the ancient ceremonial landscape integral to Stonehenge for the specific purpose of reuniting the Stones with this landscape'. 'None of the options under the Minister's consideration', it went on, 'is worthy of this site, and thus the threat to Stonehenge is now urgent, serious and imminent.' ICOMOS and the Council for British Archaeology issued a joint statement of support.

The next month an increasingly beleaguered English Heritage, caught between the conservation interests it was supposed to serve and the government that funded it, applied again to Salisbury District Council for planning permission for Denton Corker Marshall's visitor centre. The council made permission conditional on government approval for the road scheme, without which, it was felt, the centre could not be expected to function. At this point the Secretary of State called the application in and a second Stonehenge public inquiry opened on 5 December 2006. A year and a day later the government announced that the tunnel proposal was too expensive and the entire scheme, tunnels, visitor centre and all, was dropped. English Heritage pronounced itself 'very disappointed'. The Stonehenge Alliance, the National Trust, Friends of the Earth and many others were relieved. To date, the MP for Salisbury Robert Key estimates, twenty-five million pounds have been spent on proposals, consultations and inquiries. In 2008 the prospect of the 2012 London Olympics is concentrating official minds on the need to get something at least respectable in place for the anticipated influx of tourists and the Department of Culture, Media and Sport and the Department of Transport have set up a steering group. There are no plans for rerouting the roads or building a new visitor centre at this stage, but the Management Plan is being revised with a view to finding a location for a temporary visitor centre at one of more than twenty possible sites under consideration. Meanwhile among the opponents of the last scheme there has emerged a degree of consensus for a gradualist approach, for small measures, beginning with the grassing over of the A344, which might improve matters without the need for intervention on any great or irreversible scale and without prejudicing later decisions. Since such measures also have the advantage of being cheap, there is a possibility that some of them may be implemented in the not too distant future. There are those who believe and hope that the next orthodoxy to be challenged at Stonehenge will be the need always and everywhere to improve traffic flow and that the stones may prove mightier than the motor car.

In the twentieth century Stonehenge was chiefly, for good and ill, in the hands of archaeologists. In the twenty-first it has been at the mercy of administration and management. But the archaeologists have not been idle. The last seven and a half years, while they have seen almost no excavations at the site itself, have brought a number of important discoveries. Until 2002 the Stonehenge Archer was the only shadowy human figure in the prehistoric landscape. In May of that year he gained a companion of a sort when a team from Wessex Archaeology, who were digging at Amesbury, on the other side of the River Avon from Stonehenge, uncovered another, more or less contemporary grave. This, however, was a very different burial. The Amesbury Archer, as he has come to be known, was a man aged between thirty-five and forty-five, who was buried not only with arrows but with a rich array of grave goods, including five Beaker pots and two hair ornaments which are the earliest gold objects ever found in Britain. There were copper knives from France and Spain and an object that may have been an anvil, suggesting that the 'Archer' was perhaps a master craftsman, a smith from the earliest age of metal-smithing. He was also, as analysis of his teeth demonstrated, a native of the Alps, almost certainly Swiss.

He was not, as the press hoped, the king of Stonehenge. He lived too late for that and his burial across the water may suggest that those who buried him, while they treated him with great respect, saw him as a stranger to the culture of the monument. Nevertheless his grave and its contents have added a great treasure to the Salisbury Museum and another plank to the argument of those who believe in a more sophisticated and cosmopolitan prehistoric world than the archaeologists of the last century were inclined to allow. A year later the horizon became positively crowded with the arrival of the seven 'Boscombe Bowmen', whose shared grave was found at Boscombe about four miles from Stonehenge. The Bowmen were the contemporaries of the two archers and their grave included eight Beaker pots, the largest number ever found in a single grave. They were in fact three men, a teenage boy and three children, one of whom had been cremated. The skeletons of the teenager and two of the men had apparently been buried elsewhere before and brought, in part at least, for reburial at Boscombe. None of the men was native to the Stonehenge area. They may have been Welsh, which might be taken to reinforce the links between Salisbury Plain and the Preseli Hills. But they might also have come from Brittany, which may have been, Aubrey Burl has suggested, an important influence on Stonehenge, or from Portugal.

Wherever they came from, Stonehenge in its completed or at least its final form would have been a century old when they saw it. Such, at least, is the finding of the most recent research into the monument itself, which has, yet again, pushed the date back in time and compressed the period over which the several stone phases must have occurred. The work is part of the Stonehenge Riverside Project, launched in 2003 and led by Professor Mike Parker Pearson of Sheffield University, at the head of 'probably the strongest archaeological team ever assembled', along with anthropologists and the astro-archaeologist Clive Ruggles. Their work is 'focused not just on the monument, but on its landscape, its hinterland and the monuments within it' and the findings to date have been remarkable. At Stonehenge work has consisted largely of a reassessment of the conflicting evidence of the twentieth-century digs in an attempt to find a more secure date for the sarsens. Yet again William Gowland's records have proved valuable, while Richard Atkinson's were found wanting. Comparison of their notes with photographs of the excavations have enabled Parker Pearson and his colleagues to resolve apparent contradictions which seemed at one point to suggest that the outer ring was raised before the Great Trilithon, something which logic would suggest was unlikely. In fact what Atkinson took to be the erection ramp for stone 56 and on which his dating was based appears to be a later, unrelated feature. Dismissing the evidence derived from it leaves just two reliable dates for the sarsen circle and these result in a date range of 2580–2470 BC. This not only makes the sarsen stage of Stonehenge older than previously thought, it has implications for its relationship to other monuments.

This is most true of the site where Parker Pearson has been digging, Durrington Walls. This is the massive henge, about 480 yards in diameter, which lies near Woodhenge, about two miles north-east of Stonehenge itself. In 1967, despite protests from archaeologists, the road through Durrington Walls was straightened, destroying much of it. Before work began, however, Geoffrey Wainwright oversaw large, high-speed excavations, taking bulldozers to the site in a manner that shocked some of his colleagues but yielded valuable if tantalising information about what Durrington had looked like and how it might have been used. Two circles of post holes were revealed and the latest digs have found evidence of more. They have also shown an avenue leading to the river, similar to that at Stonehenge though much shorter. It was about thirty-three yards wide, surfaced with rammed flint, animal bones and pottery and had been heavily trampled in the middle. Whatever Durrington was used for, it was used by many people.

The discovery that captured public imagination in 2006, however, was the foundations of houses within the enclosure and outside it beside the avenue. The houses were small but would have been comfortable, with clay floors, oval central hearths and in two cases beam slots for wooden box beds built in against the walls. They may have been occupied only seasonally and they may possibly have been what the press wanted them to be, a construction workers' village for the labour force building Stonehenge, but none of that is certain. What is clear, from the number of pig bones, the almost complete absence of human bones and the other finds at the site, is that Durrington Walls was inhabited and was a secular rather than a purely ritual site. The new dates for Stonehenge make the two contemporary, prompting questions about their relationship. Of the two circles discovered by Wainwright at Durrington, the southern one has now been more fully explored using magnetometry and ground-penetrating radar, which shows a ground plan with an inner oval that closely resembles Stonehenge in the later part of Phase Three. Clive

Ruggles has established that this southern Durrington circle is 'aligned precisely on the midwinter sunrise, corresponding almost exactly to the upper limb of the winter solstice sun in 3000–2500 BC'. Not only does this strike another blow for astro-archaeology, it establishes an elegant and compelling link between Durrington and Stonehenge. Stonehenge is aligned on the midsummer sunrise and midwinter sunset, the Durrington circle complements it, facing the midsummer sunset and midwinter sunrise. This makes it seem likely that the same people used both places.

At Stonehenge itself the very latest findings of Parker Pearson's team, announced in 2008, date the Aubrey Holes, those most mysterious features, securely to Phase One. They also prove that Stonehenge was used for burials, mostly cremations, throughout its existence until 2450 BC, adding weight to the idea of it as a place essentially associated with the dead. 'I'm very pleased', Parker Pearson noted, 'it seems to have been a cemetery all the way through. The small numbers (about 240 buried over 500 years from 2950 BC to 2450 BC) suggest that it was a pretty exclusive group of men, women and children, so it may have been something equivalent to a royal burial ground.' This is the latest theory, suggestive but unprovable. It fits with the other most popular current archaeological view of Stonehenge as a site of ancestor worship. This suggestion derives from Parker Pearson's colleague the Madagascan archaeologist Ramilisonina, who took one look at the stones and had no hesitation in pronouncing that it was 'blindingly obvious' that 'this is all for the ancestors'. By analogy with Madagascar, he saw in Stonehenge, where a wooden structure is transformed into stone, a monument to the once-living, now venerated in death. This idea has been taken up by Mike Pitts and Parker Pearson himself. Yet while the contrast between Durrington and Stonehenge as places of life and of death, or at least secular and sacred, looks likely, there is no evidence for ancestor worship per se. Many cultures have death rites that do not involve deification of the dead. The contrast between wood and stone may be as much practical as metaphorical, a contrast between short- and long-term constructions. Any medieval city, after all, was built on the same principle, with timber-framed houses surrounding the stone cathedral. Elsewhere the idea of the 'hospital', the healing stones, is still very much alive. The first dig of the new millennium, the first in fact for forty-four years, was undertaken in March and April 2008 by the main proponents of the theory, Geoffrey Wainwright and Tim Darvill. They investigated the site of the first bluestone structure in the hope of finding further evidence and Darvill also suggested, more controversially, that their work may herald a return to excavation at Stonehenge.

To Mike Pitts the sarsen stones are also sculpture, giant versions of the flaked implements used by Stone Age builders: 'an arrangement of absurdly massive stone tools … Taking a small everyday object, using everyday technology, but in ways previously unimagined, people created something on an unprecedented scale … expanding scale does more than just make something bigger. Handled with skill it can transform the banal into the awesome.' How intentional such a resemblance was and whether, several millennia before Pop Art, such a concept could really have existed, is debatable. Among the other possibilities that continue to float like bubbles to the surface of the media is the idea put forward in 2003 by Anthony Perks, a gynaecologist at the University of British

Columbia, a fertility theory that allowed the *Observer* newspaper to run a story headlined 'The vagina monoliths: Stonehenge was ancient sex symbol'.

The Stonehenge of the new millennium reflects, as ever, the age that shapes it. While archaeologists in the nineteenth and earlier twentieth centuries, when Britain still had an empire, tended to interpret the past in terms of violence and conquest, the post imperial age has thought more about influence. The Beaker People have turned from an invading race to a cultural shift and Parker Pearson's findings suggest that the Beaker culture was in Wessex earlier than had been thought. The 'howling barbarians' of Atkinson's day are, in an age of multiculturalism, seen as less bloodthirsty and more worthy of respect. The skull of the child buried at Woodhenge, once assumed to have been violently split in half in an act of human sacrifice, is now thought merely to have fallen apart during decomposition. It may not even be contemporary with Woodhenge. On a practical level, relations between the authorities, the Druids and the counterculture are, for the moment, harmonious, although the sad death of Tim Sebastian, founder of the Secular Order of Druids, in 2007 occasioned some tension over the question of whether his ashes could be scattered at Stonehenge. Elsewhere modern Druidry is thriving and the orders continue to multiply and divide. Since 1990 five or six a year have emerged on average, although the rumoured Police Lodge of Druids, PLOD, has so far failed to materialise. In 2002 Rowan Williams, as Archbishop of Canterbury designate, was initiated into the Gorsedd of Bards and was 'saddened', though he should not have been surprised, when this aroused vigorous protests and allegations of paganism at the heart of the established

34. Watching for the sunrise, 2006. Since 2000 the public has been able to celebrate the summer solstice from inside the stones under English Heritage's policy of 'managed open access', which has so far proved popular and successful.

Church. The midsummer solstice celebrations continue to grow, while increasing awareness of the importance of the winter solstice brings ever greater numbers to the stones in December. English Heritage has allowed spectators inside the fence for the sunrise, which in 2007 attracted several hundred people, including Druids of several orders, drummers, pipers and photographers. By contrast the sunset on the shortest day, which seems more securely linked to the intentions of the builders of Stonehenge, remains almost unmarked.

It is impossible to think about Stonehenge for any length of time without formulating a theory and so, having tried to deal fairly with the various ideas, visions and beliefs that have emanated from the stones throughout recorded history, I cannot resist concluding with a thought of my own, deduced from the research of Parker Pearson and his team. Although the archaeologists have not spelled it out in quite these terms, we might see Stonehenge as marking the beginning and the end of the darkest months of the year, while Durrington celebrates the light, the high point of summer and the turn away from midwinter. So perhaps, twice a year, at midsummer and midwinter, the inhabitants of Durrington, who were also the worshippers at Stonehenge, would have gone from one place to the other. Midsummer Eve at Durrington would be followed by dawn at Stonehenge as the year turned from light towards dark, while in midwinter the procession would go the other way, from Stonehenge at sunset on the shortest day to dawn at Durrington, to see the light return. It is a possibility, one more image to add to all the changing scenes the centuries have projected on to the mute, mysterious stones.

PLANNING A VISIT?

Despite the poor facilities at the 'national disgrace' of a visitor centre, Stonehenge itself never disappoints. It is located just off the A344, but for those who want to avoid adding to the traffic problems that so beset it the nearest railway station is Salisbury, 9 miles away, and the Wiltshire and Dorset Bus Company's service no. 3 runs to Stonehenge. The site is open all year except Christmas, but opening hours vary according to the hours of daylight. Summer opening (1 June to 31 August) is 9 a.m. to 7 p.m., with last admission half an hour before closing time. Most visitors stop on the path and look towards the stones, but don't forget to look outwards as well to take in the whole site, including the bank, the ditch and the markers showing the Aubrey Holes, in addition to the wider landscape. The sites of the Mesolithic post holes, the earliest known man-made features, are marked by white concrete circles in the car park and it is worth making motorists wait while you stand on them to assess their relationship to Stonehenge itself.

Outside normal visiting hours it is sometimes possible to arrange special access to the stones. Contact English Heritage with enquiries. For the summer solstice, arrangements are, as the EH website puts it laconically, 'subject to change'.

Look out for detailed information nearer the time about what the conditions will be for any given year. The Wiltshire and Dorset Bus Company's website also gives details of its regular service to and from Salisbury station throughout the night. The winter solstice is growing in popularity. It is not possible (or for most people desirable) to spend the night at Stonehenge in December, but in recent years there has been an arrangement for public access to see the sunrise from within the circle. The crowds are smaller than in the summer, so it is easier to get to the stones and you will also see a higher proportion of Druids (of one sort or another) in the winter. Midsummer is now too crowded for many of them. There are so far no special arrangements for the midwinter sunset but it occurs during ordinary opening hours and can be seen – if it is visible at all – from the path.

The World Heritage Site covers 96,500 acres in all and if you have a day, or more, to explore it there is a great deal to be seen. Some areas are administered by English Heritage; the rest belongs to the National Trust, the Ministry of Defence and various farmers and private householders. The Great Cursus is on National Trust land and is accessible, but the Lesser Cursus is not. Woodhenge is an English Heritage site and access to it is free. The positions of the original posts are marked by colour-coded concrete pillars. You will often have the site to yourself and it is a good place to stand and feel something of the quietness of the landscape that is missing at Stonehenge. Durrington Walls is visible from the Woodhenge car park and partially accessible, as is the field just to the south of it, which has the cuckoo stone in it, an isolated sarsen whose purpose is unclear but is now being explored as part of the Stonehenge Riverside Project. Of the barrows many can be reached or at least seen from nearby paths and bridleways. They include Kings Barrow Ridge and some of the Normanton Down and Winterbourne Stoke Crossroads groups as well as Bush Barrow. At the time of writing, the National Trust is working to make more of its land to the west of Stonehenge accessible and hopes to achieve this by 2009. Coneybury Henge is on farmland and is not now visible on the ground, but the whole of Stonehenge Down is accessible. Avebury belongs to the National Trust.

Most of the archaeological finds from Stonehenge are now in the Salisbury and South Wiltshire Museum, which is in the King's House, no. 65 in the Cathedral Close at Salisbury. The King's House is a medieval and Elizabethan building that features in Hardy's *Jude the Obscure* and is well worth visiting for its own sake. Open from Monday to Saturday, it is also now the home of the Amesbury and Stonehenge Archers and of objects varying from an exquisite macehead, made of polished gneiss, to the humble antler picks of the workers who dug the Stonehenge ditch. Visit the museum after you have been to the stones. Objects which seem dull or enigmatic in isolation become immediate and moving when you have just come from the monument itself.

A little further away, at 41 Long Street, Devizes, is the Devizes Museum, home of the Wiltshire Archaeological and Natural History Society and spiritual home of the antiquarian pursuit of Stonehenge. Its prime exhibit (and indeed its first acquisition) is John Britton's Celtic Cabinet. In addition to this the museum holds many of William Cunnington's finds, including the beautiful collection from Upton Lovell, the early Bronze Age 'Golden Barrow', as well as a rich collection of watercolours and engravings of Stonehenge and other

Wiltshire sites from the eighteenth century to the present day. The museum is open every day and the library, which holds a large collection related to Stonehenge, as well as many of John Britton's papers, can be visited by appointment.

FURTHER READING

INTRODUCTION

For a general study of Stonehenge in history and prehistory the best book by far is *Stonehenge Complete*, by Christopher Chippindale (London, 1983). Chippindale is an archaeologist whose own career has become part of the Stonehenge story over the last three decades. He is impatient with Druids, architects and others who fail to anticipate field archaeology, but he has an unrivalled grasp of the material and writes with great lucidity and humour. His title proved something of a hostage to fortune, however, and the book was republished in 2004 in a revised and expanded edition. Julian Richards's *Stonehenge: the Story So Far* (Swindon, 2007) is the most up-to-date overall survey of the archaeology and the history.

ARCHAEOLOGY

Stonehenge in Its Landscape: Twentieth-century excavations, by Rosamund M. J. Cleal, K. E. Walker and R. Montague, published by English Heritage (London, 1995), is the monumental founding text of modern Stonehenge studies, bringing together for the first time all the surviving archaeological records. It led directly to *Science and Stonehenge* (Oxford, 1997), edited by Barry Cunliffe and Colin Renfrew, which comprises papers given at a British Academy conference on various aspects of *Stonehenge in Its Landscape*. *Science and Stonehenge* has contributions by archaeologists, engineers, astro-archaeologists, geologists and environmentalists and includes a study of possible construction techniques. Both volumes are fairly heavy going. For a scholarly but less dense archaeological account of Stonehenge and the culture to which it belonged go to *Hengeworld* by Mike Pitts (London, 2000), a gripping read which reconstructs the ancient world in vivid detail by the light of the late twentieth-century discoveries at and near Stonehenge. Pitts has his own theories to offer, as has Aubrey Burl, whose *Stonehenge: A New History of the World's Greatest Stone Circle* (London, 2006) is a persuasive but contentious account. Burl is a leading expert on stone circles and he argues for a strong Breton influence on Salisbury Plain. He is also the main, if not now the only, proponent of the theory that the bluestones arrived on Salisbury Plain as a result of glaciation. For children *The Amazing Pop-Up Stonehenge*, by Julian Richards and Linda Birkinshaw (Swindon, 2005), tells the story as simply as possible and allows readers to put up a sarsen at the mere pull of a paper tab.

HISTORY AND ANTIQUARIANISM

The History of the Kings of Britain, by Geoffrey of Monmouth, was published in Penguin Classics (Harmondsworth, 1976). Lewis Thorpe, who translated it, also contributed a long and compelling introduction that puts Geoffrey in context and discusses the meaning of history in the Middle Ages. A new edition, translated by Neil Wright and edited by Michael

Reeve (Rochester, NY) was published in 2007. *The Anglia Historia of Polydore Vergil* (London, 1950) also has an excellent introduction by Denys Hays. Lucas de Heere's watercolour is discussed in 'Lucas de Heere's Stonehenge', by J. A. Bakker, *Antiquity*, LIII (1979), 107–11, and *Chorea Gigantum…*, by Walter Charleton (London, 1663), was reprinted with Jones's and Webb's treatises as a single volume in 1775. The two twentieth-century editions of this volume are discussed under 'Architects'.

John Aubrey's vast and rambling manuscripts have never attracted the team of scholars they need – and deserve – to produce a fully annotated edition. *Monumenta Britannica, John Aubrey, Part 3*, edited by Rodney Legg and John Fowles (Sherborne, Dorset, 1982), which reproduces his Stonehenge study, is, however, very much better than nothing. *John Aubrey and the Realm of Learning*, by Michael Hunter (London, 1975), is an intellectual biography. For a briefer but vivid account of his life and remarkable character I recommend 'John Aubrey' in *The Trophies of Time: English Antiquarians of the Seventeenth Century*, by Graham Parry (Oxford, 1995). This collection of essays opens up the world of antiquarianism with humour as well as erudition and also includes 'Phoenicia Britannica', a rare study of Aylett Sammes.

William Stukeley has attracted a considerable modern literature in addition to his own *Stonehenge A Temple Restor'd to the Druids* (London, 1740). '"A small journey into the country": William Stukeley and the Formal Landscapes of Stonehenge and Avebury', by David Haycock, in *Producing the Past: Aspects of Antiquarian Culture and Practice 1700–1850*, edited by Martin Myrone and Lucy Peltz (Aldershot, 1999), demonstrates elegantly the connection between Stukeley's view of Stonehenge and the landscape art of his age. David Haycock followed it with his biography, *William Stukeley: Science, Religion and Archaeology in Eighteenth-century England* (Woodbridge, 2002). As a historian Haycock sees Stukeley in context and is able to accommodate both his archaeological and his religious views in a consistent account. The archaeological riposte to Haycock came in *Stukeley's 'Stonehenge': An Unpublished Manuscript 1721–24*, edited by Aubrey Burl and Neil Mortimer (New Haven and London, 2005), which has an introduction arguing that Stukeley's reason was undermined by his ordination as an Anglican clergyman. A middle way between the two is suggested in 'The Religion of William Stukeley', by Ronald Hutton, *Antiquaries Journal*, 85 (2005), which considers Stukeley's religious ideas throughout his life.

The literature on the Druids is vast and ever expanding but *The Famous Druids*, by A. L. Owen (Oxford, 1962), which covers 'three centuries of English Literature on the Druids', is still the best introduction. *The Druids*, by Stuart Piggott (Harmondsworth, 1974), is a scholarly if occasionally bad-tempered account of ancient and modern Druidry, while *The Druids*, by Ronald Hutton (London, 2007), takes a deeper and more forgiving overview of old and new Druids and their cultural significance and can be profitably read in conjunction with *The Image of Antiquity, Ancient Britain and the Romantic Imagination*, by Sam Smiles (New Haven and London, 1994) and Rosemary Sweet's *Antiquaries: The discovery of the past in eighteenth-century Britain* (London, 2004).

The Margate shell grotto has a website, www.shellgrotto. co.uk, which gives details of its possible history and its opening times. It was also the inspiration for *The Realm of Shells*, a novel by Sheila Overall (London, 2006).

The 1725 edition of Inigo Jones's *The Most Notable Antiquity of Great Britain, vulgarly called Stone-heng on Salisbury Plain Restored* (including Charleton's and Webb's treatises) was published in a facsimile edition by Gregg International in 1971. It has a discouraging Introduction, by Stuart Piggott, that promises only 'a forgotten controversy on forgotten lines of argument'. In 1972 the Scolar Press retaliated with another facsimile edition introduced by Graham Parry, who enters with more sympathy and knowledge into the debate and its intellectual context. The best introduction to Jones's work overall is still John Summerson's *Inigo Jones* (New Haven and London, republished 2000). *Britannia Triumphans: Inigo Jones, Rubens and Whitehall Palace*, by Roy Strong (London, 1980), discusses the iconography of the Banqueting Hall ceiling and its relation to Jones's other ideas. Jones's intellectual status is the subject of 'Inigo Jones, Architect and Man of Letters', in *The Collected Essays of Rudolf Wittkower: Palladio and English Palladianism* (London, 1974). The classical sources for *Stone-heng* are discussed in detail in 'Inigo Jones's Stone-Heng', by A. A. Tait, *Burlington Magazine*, 120, 900 (March 1978), 154–9, and the connections between Jones's theories about Stonehenge, his theatrical work and the memory theatres of the Renaissance are discussed in 'Public Theatre and Masque: Inigo Jones on the Theatre as a Temple', Chapter Ten of *Theatre of the World*, by Frances Yates (Chicago, 1969).

John Wood's *Choir Gaure, vulgarly called Stonehenge on Salisbury Plain Described, Restored and Explained*, was published in Oxford in 1747. His *The Origin of Building: or, the Plagiarism of the Heathens Detected* (1741) was republished in a facsimile edition by Gregg International in 1968. John

Summerson's essay 'John Wood and the English Town-Planning Tradition', in his *Heavenly Mansions* (London, 1949), was the first critical study of Wood and although outdated in some points, especially in its account of his life, is full of acute observations. The most extensive study of Wood's life and work is *John Wood: Architect of Obsession*, by Tim Mowl and Brian Earnshaw (Bath, 1988), though a more perceptive critique of his thinking is to be found in Eileen Harris's 'John Wood's System of Architecture', *Burlington Magazine*, 131, 1031 (February 1989), 101–7. *Obsession: John Wood and the Creation of Georgian Bath* (Bath, 2004) is a small but well-illustrated exhibition catalogue comprising essays on many aspects of Wood and his career. George Wither's *A Collection of Emblemes Ancient and Modern* (1635) was reprinted with a scholarly introduction by Rosemary Freeman (South Carolina, 1975). There is a discussion of Soane's interest in Stonehenge in Peter Thornton and Helen Dorey's *A Miscellany of Objects from Sir John Soane's Museum* (London, 1992). Derek Walker's *The Architecture and Planning of Milton Keynes* (London, 1982) tells the official story of the town's development and includes some of the more far-out unbuilt designs.

ROMANTICS

A facsimile edition of Blake's *Jerusalem*, with an introduction and notes by Morton D. Paley, was published by Princeton in 1991 and Peter D. Fisher explores the subject of 'Blake and the Druids' in the *Journal of English and Germanic Philology*, LVIII (1959), 589–612. For a masterly and detailed critical discussion of both Wordsworth and Blake in this context see Anne Janowitz's *England's Ruins: Poetic Purpose and the*

National Landscape (Cambridge, Mass., and Oxford, 1990), and for a list of poems on Stonehenge and other monuments see *Topographic Poetry in Eighteenth-century England*, by Robert Arnold Aubin (New York, 1936). 'Iolo Morganwg and the Romantic Tradition in Wales' is now the subject of an extensive publishing project currently being undertaken by the University of Wales under the general editorship of Geraint H. Jenkins. They have so far published: *A Rattleskull Genius: The Many Faces of Iolo Morganwygg*, edited by Geraint H. Jenkins; *Bardic Circles: National Regional and Personal Identity in the Bardic Vision of Iolo Morganwygg*, by Catherine A. Charnell-White; and *The Truth Against the World: Iolo Morganwyg and Romantic Forgery*, by Mary-Ann Constantine (Cardiff).

John Britton's plans for the Druidical Antiquarian Company appeared in the *Gentleman's Magazine* for December 1825 and his Celtic Cabinet is fully discussed by Christopher Chippindale in 'John Britton's "Celtic Cabinet" in Devizes Museum and its Context', *Antiquaries Journal*, LXV, Part One (1985), 121–38. The plans for the light show form part of the discussion in 'Megalithic Follies: Soane's "Druidic Remains" and the Display of Monuments', by Christopher Evans, *Journal of Modern Culture*, 5 (2000), 347–66. Scott Paul Gordon's analysis of the meaning of James Barry's painting is in 'Reading Patriot Art: James Barry's *King Lear*', in *Eighteenth-century Studies*, 36, 4 (2003), 491–509, and the evolution of Constable's watercolour is discussed in *Constable's Stonehenge* by Louis Hawes (London, 1975).

The 'Sarum Plain' section of Coventry Patmore's *Angel in the House* is in Canto VIII of Book One, written in 1854. Recent years have seen a greatly increased interest in the Victorians and their reaction to evolutionary theory. For Charles Lyell and his influence I relied on James Secord's introduction to the Penguin Classics edition of *Principles of Geology* (London, 1997), as well as his brilliantly detailed and far-reaching analysis, *Victorian Sensation: The Extraordinary Publication, Reception, and Secret Authorship of Vestiges of the Natural History of Creation* (London and Chicago, 2000). The literature on Darwin himself is vast. Perhaps the best way into it is via Janet Browne's two-volume biography, *Voyaging* and *The Power of Place* (London, 1995 and 2002), and her *Darwin's Origin of Species, a Biography* (London, 2006). *Darwin's Plots* by Gillian Beer (second edition, Cambridge, 2000), examines the influence of evolutionary theory on Victorian novelists, including Hardy and George Eliot; while Elizabeth Jay's *Faith and Doubt in Victorian Britain* (London, 1986) takes a broader view of the impact of science on religious belief.

The Establishment of Human Antiquity, by Donald K. Grayson (New York and London, 1983), gives a detailed account of that debate and Robert F. Heizer's 'The Background of Thomsen's Three-Age System', *Technology and Culture*, 3, 3 (Summer, 1962), 259–66, shows how the archaeological account of prehistory emerged. The history of archaeology itself as a separate discipline is covered by Glyn Daniel's *A Short History of Archaeology* (London, 1981) and *The History of Archaeology* by John Romer (London, 2001). John Herschel's camera lucida drawing was published for the first time in 'John Herschel Visits Stonehenge', by Howard Mitchell,

British Archaeology (July/August 2007), 50–51, where comparison with a modern photograph shows clearly how the stones which fell in 1900 were restored at a slightly different angle. The troubled later nineteenth-century history of Stonehenge is told in full in 'The enclosure of Stonehenge', by Christopher Chippindale, *Wiltshire Archaeological Magazine*, 70–71 for 1975–6 (1978), 109–23. *Preservation*, by Wayland Kennet (London, 1972), deals with the history and culture of conservation. Michael Hunter's Introduction to a collection of essays, *Preserving the Past: The Rise of Heritage in Modern Britain* (Stroud, 1996), discusses the first conservation legislation. 'Is Anyone Minding Stonehenge? The Origins of Cultural Property Protection in England', by Joseph L. Sax, *California Law Review*, 78, 6 (December 1990), 1543–67, analyses attitudes to private property and the moral implications of the legislation.

ARCHAEOLOGY, ASTRONOMY AND THE AGE OF AQUARIUS

A Sentimental and Practical Guide to Amesbury and Stonehenge compiled by Lady Antrobus (1900) was the first guidebook of the twentieth century after the fence had gone up. *The Gate of Remembrance*, by F. Bligh Bond (Oxford, 1918), describes his Glastonbury seances. John Piper's caustic account of his disappointing visit was published as 'Stonehenge' in the *Architectural Review*, 106 (1949), 177–82. *England and the Octopus* (London, 1928) and *On Trust for the Nation* (London, 1949), both by Clough Williams-Ellis, place Stonehenge in the context of pre- and post-war landscape, and two of Paul Nash's Avebury-inspired paintings, *Landscape of the Megaliths* and *Equivalents for the Megaliths*, are in Tate Britain in London.

The revival of interest in Alfred Watkins and his ideas is discussed in 'Notes Towards a Social History of Ley-hunting' by Roger Sandell, based on 'a talk given largely extempore, at the Anglo-French UFO meeting held at Hove in March 1988', in *Magonia*, 29 (April 1988). The reputation of William Gowland has been steadily rising in recent years, largely due to the research of Simon Kaner. His 'William Gowland (1842–1922): Pioneer of Japanese Archaeology' appeared in *Britain and Japan: Biographical Portraits*, Vol. VI, edited by H. Cortazzi (Folkstone, 2007).

The modern astronomical accounts of Stonehenge begin with *Stonehenge and Other British Stone Monuments Astronomically Considered*, by Sir Norman Lockyer (1906; second edition, London, 1909) and the debate starts with *Stonehenge Decoded*, by Gerald S. Hawkins in collaboration with John B. White (London, 1966). Hawkins's book is easy to read if less easy, on reflection, to understand. 'Moonshine on Stonehenge', by Richard Atkinson, *Antiquity* (September 1966), was one of the first refutations of Hawkins's case and does at least engage with the arguments. *On Stonehenge*, by Fred Hoyle (London, 1977), contains the articles previously published in *Antiquity* on the astronomical implications and is difficult to follow without some specialist knowledge. In *Secrets of the Stones: The Story of Astro-archaeology* (Harmondsworth, 1977) John Michell takes a lucid if particular view of the whole debate as it reflects on human beings, ancient and modern. His *The View over Atlantis* (London, 1969) was the manifesto of the earth mysteries movement. John North's *Stonehenge: Neolithic Man and the Cosmos* (London, 1996), described as 'a controversial throwback', surveys the astronomical arguments from the point of view of a historian of science and is a dense but interesting read. The best and least partial academic study of the whole subject is *Astronomy in Prehistoric Britain and Ireland*, by Clive Ruggles (New Haven and London, 1999), which discusses the ideas and their fraught history with fairness and humour. The story of the counterculture on Salisbury Plain is told in Andy Worthington's witty and well-researched *Stonehenge: Celebration and Subversion* (Loughborough, 2004). The Stonehenge sequence from *Spinal Tap* is on YouTube (www.youtube.com).

Outdated in some ways and overshadowed by the decline in his professional reputation, Richard Atkinson's *Stonehenge* (Pelican edition, Harmondsworth, 1960) is nevertheless still a good read, a model, however flawed, of popular science writing. The recent troubles on Salisbury Plain were first tackled in print by Christopher Chippindale, who edited *Who Owns Stonehenge?* (London, 1990). *The Trials of Arthur: The Life and Times of a Modern-day King*, by Arthur Pendragon and Christopher James Stone (London, 2003), tells the story of Arthur's remarkable life as a man and as an absurdist figure of protest. 'Stonehenge: The Saga Continues', by Elizabeth Young and Wayland Kennet, *Journal of Architectural Conservation*, 3 (November 2000), 70–85, recounts attempts to improve the site up to the millennium. To take the story further see *The Stonehenge Saga*, available on the Council for British Archaeology website, www.britarch.ac.uk, which brings events up to the present with links to other relevant sites and documents. *The A303 Stonehenge Improvement Review* is available as a PDF download in two parts from the Highways Agency website, www.highways.gov.uk.

'The Age of Stonehenge', *Antiquity* (September 2007), 617–39, by Mike Parker Pearson and thirteen others, is the most recent publication on the current research. News of current developments and discussions can be found in many places on the internet but the website www.savestonehenge. org.uk is probably a good place to start.

LIST OF ILLUSTRATIONS

ACKNOWLEDGEMENTS

I am grateful to Dave Batchelor of English Heritage, who cast an expert archaeologist's eye over parts of the text and arranged for me to visit Stonehenge outside public opening hours, and to Mike Parker Pearson, who kindly shared his latest findings with me. Anne Janowitz and Gavin Stamp read parts of the book and commented on it constructively. Neil Mortimer helped me with images from Stukeley's *Stonehenge*; Jan Piggott scanned his copy of Turner's engraving and Calista Lucy delivered it to me. Jeremy Harte of the Bourne Hall Museum, Surrey, gave an inspiring lecture on John Aubrey and fairy tradition which prompted useful trains of thought and he patiently answered my questions afterwards; Michael Hall directed my reading on Lyell and Darwin; Larry Schaaf and Howard Mitchell told me about Herschel's drawing of Stonehenge and Fox Talbot's failure to photograph it; Andrew Mahaddie recalled his experiences of working on Milton Keynes and kindly allowed me to reproduce his drawing; Louis Hellman let me republish his cartoon; Ellis Woodman passed on James Gowan's remarks about the Churchill College competition and Lucy Evershed and Stephen Fisher of the National Trust helped with information about the Trust's holdings and their history.

INDEX

Y

Yates, Dame Frances 1
Yeats, W. B. 134
'Y' holes 16, 152
York Minster 83

Z

'Z' holes 16, 152

WONDERS OF THE WORLD

This is a small series of books, under the general editorship of
Mary Beard, that will focus on some of the world's most famous
sites or monuments.